MW00526229

# My Crazy Life

## AISHA P. FELIX

**My Crazy Life**
Copyright © 2021 Aisha P. Felix

Produced and printed by Stillwater River Publications.
All rights reserved. Written and produced in the
United States of America. This book may not be reproduced
or sold in any form without the expressed, written
permission of the author and publisher.

Visit our website at
www.StillwaterPress.com
for more information.

First Stillwater River Publications Edition.

ISBN: 978-1-955123-21-1

1 2 3 4 5 6 7 8 9 10
Written by Aisha P. Felix
Pawtucket, RI, USA.

*The views and opinions expressed*
*in this book are solely those of the author*
*and do not necessarily re lect the views*
*and opinions of the publisher.*

# DEDICATION

To:
*My son who has brought meaning to my life and my motivation to live. He has encouraged me to do what I love to do and taught me to not give up in life.*

*This book is also dedicated to the memory of my grandfather, Rudolph Felix. My grandfather was a present to the world, a man who knew the true meaning of family.*

*For the people who are struggling with depression or any mental illness. I pray you find the courage and strength to keep going, do not give up. I hope you find the support you need.*

# Contents

# *Introduction*

On August 15th, 2017, I waited to be discharged from the mental health unit at Saint Claire's Hospital. The psychiatrist invited me into his office before I left. The psychiatrist said that I was not treated for what I have which is bipolar disorder. He prescribed 600 milligrams of Lithium then asked if I had ever considered electroshock treatment. What was this doctor trying to do, fry my brain? Was this the solution to my mental illness?

Reminiscing about my life, I never imagined being in this state called Rhode Island. I had trials, triumphs, and I was trapped in a life I disliked. I felt God resigned from hearing my prayers. I contemplated and attempted suicide numerous times; however on August 9th 2017, I had a more specific plan in mind. My plan led me to Saint Claire's Hospital. At the hospital, a girl accompanied my roommate and I to our lunch table. The girl placed a book on the table and told me that this self-help book titled *You are a Badass* had helped her. The title caught my interest and I bought the book after I was released from the hospital.

On page 12 of her book, *You are a Badass*, author Jen Sincero points out, "You need to go from wanting to change your life to deciding to change your life." The author then asks, "What have you been saying forever that you'd love to do?" I pondered the words and I realized that I love to write. I have kept journals all my life; however, I have never written a book. Her words lingered in my head and I took the author's advice and went from wanting to deciding to write this book. Everyone has a story to tell, I chose to tell mine.

Maya Angelou once said, "There is no greater agony than bearing an untold story inside you."

I considered different titles for this book such as: *My Battle with Depression*, *Learning How to Survive*, and *A Cry for Help*. Only one title summarized my life in three words. Will this book make a difference? I am unaware if this book will make a difference; however, I would like to share the story with you of... 'My Crazy Life.'

*My Crazy Life*

# CHAPTER 1

# In the Beginning

*I* knew the world was harsh from the moment I exited my mother's womb. The nurse slapped me on the butt because I did not cry. My mother was also informed that I was a boy during her pregnancy and received baby boy clothing at her baby shower. I am also sure I was dropped on the head a few times, too.

My name is Aisha Patrisha Felix, born on the twenty-eighth of August on a gloomy Wednesday morning. I was born at the Charlotte Amalie Hospital in Saint Thomas, United States Virgin Islands. At the age of eighteen months I was sent to live with relatives in Dominica. In Dominica. I lived with my aunt and her husband on the Morne Saint Joseph. At the age of two, I almost died of a seizure known as The Fits. My father panicked and took me to a witch doctor who lived nearby. My father mentioned that I was unresponsive and the woman saved my life.

I was an active toddler growing up and knew my aunt was my mother, yet I felt I was nobody's child. I received no mommy kisses nor daddy's smile. This song, "Nobody's Child" by Karen

Young always made me cry. The song reminded me of how I felt. I grew up with the belief that my mother abandoned me and I grew up without a father. When I was twelve years old my grandmother reminded my father he had a daughter. After that conversation with my grandmother, my father visited me every October. My cousin Kayler and I lived together until she left Dominica in 1994 at around the age of eight years old. My aunt in New York left her in the care of my aunt in Dominica to seek a better life for both she and her daughter.

My family was religious and I was taught to live according to the lessons of the Bible. My family tried to live by the Ten Commandments. What I heard often was, "Do not swear, to obey is better than to sacrifice, I should refrain from taking God's name in vain, and spare the rod spoil the child. My grandmother taught me that a person could only raise their hands to me if that person feeds me. I was raised with manners and to only go places I was invited.

My whole life was scheduled every day of the week. Mondays and Tuesdays were normal school days and Wednesday evenings my family and I attended prayer meetings at church. The only book I could read on Wednesday night was the Bible. My Harlequin romance and Sweet Valley High and Sweet Valley University books would wait for another day. On Thursday evenings I attended choir practice at church and worshipped on Friday evenings. My family were Seventh Day Adventist and went to church on Saturdays, except for my Catholic grandmother. My family was not rich, still I am humble to say I was more fortunate than some children.

Children have cellular phones and game systems today. As a kid growing up, my entertainment was Barbie dolls, crayon books, embroidery and watching television. I also had a Cabbage Patch doll and my cousin had a Chucky doll that she used to scare kids at school. Schools in Dominica were different from the United States. Children had less technology and more structure in Dominica.

In Dominica, growing up, I was always happy to find a quarter under my pillow when my aunt pretended to be the tooth fairy. Santa Claus never got credit for the gifts I received at Christmas. I remembered my aunt in New York sent beautiful dresses for my cousin and I at Christmas. Christmas was best spent with my grandmother. I believe every child's favorite holiday is Christmas. My grandmother's husband made sure the fridge was filled with apples for me. He was a hard-working man who always found something to do, similar to my father.

My aunt and grandmother who raised me taught me the importance of education, discipline, spiritual life, and the value of family. I believe my family raised me the best way they knew how. To prevent confusion with another country, let me tell you about where I grew up.

# CHAPTER 2

# Where I Grew Up

"No matter how far you go in life,
never forget where you come from."
— *Titus Hoskins*

*H*ow could I forget the culture, language, food, traditions and customs of Dominica? Most of the enjoyable experiences in my life I had in this Isle of Beauty, Dominica. To avoid confusion with the Dominican Republic, the Commonwealth of Dominica is located between two French countries: Martinique and Guadeloupe.

Like most Dominicans, the people of my village grow their own food for their own consumption. They raised animals such as goats, pigs, sheep, chickens and some cows. My Uncle Alfred had his own garden where he grew ground provisions such as bananas, plantain, dasheen, figs, vegetables and fruits. The fruits were never processed; any fruit you obtained you could have picked from a tree. I remembered I picked lemons, guavas, mangos, sugar apples, and soursop from trees. My aunt told me to ask for permission before taking fruit from anyone's tree. My aunt made juice from lemons and cherries and made jam or jelly with the guavas. Guava juice and home squeezed lemonade were my favorite.

The crops my uncle collected were brought to my grand-mother to cook. We enjoyed the plantain, fig, and roasted dasheen fried or boiled. I preferred roasted breadfruit and plantain roasted on a coal pot. Thanks to my grandmother who cooked the food, it was cooked to perfection. I believed that if my grandmother were to pass away, the world would cease to exist. The sun would refuse to shine, the moon would lose its light; plants would cease to grow without my grandmother. My grandmother held the family together. My grandmother pre-pared the meals and had them distributed to members of our family in our village.

My village, Saint Joseph, was a small village. Everyone in the community had their own housing ranging from wood and brick houses with large porches. No apartment complex was in sight. People socialized at shops, churches, or on the street. My uncle had a bar attached to his house where he sold goods and other items. Most customers socialized at my uncle's bar.

What I missed in Dominica are the traditions of New Year's Day, Independence Day (Creole Day), and Carnival.

During New Year's, my grandmother bought a fresh live goat then brought it home to be used for the holiday season.

My grandmother blessed the goat and slaughtered it in a specific way. I know that sounds harsh; however, that was tra-dition. After the goat was slaughtered, my grandmother made soup with the goat called goat water. Never mind what the name sounds like. When the soup entered your mouth the soup was like a touch of heaven. This palatable meal was *très bien* (very good). Along with this delicious meal we had a seasonal drink called sorrel. The sorrel is peeled and the leaves are boiled with cinnamon, clove, and ginger, then sweetened. The holidays were always a spectacular one with family and guests who often visited.

Another holiday is Carnival celebrated in February or March each year on a Monday and Tuesday before Ash Wednesday. The village was lively with Calypso music, costumes, and celebrations. My aunt Eleanor and her husband Steve who I lived with shared the Seventh Day Adventist faith; therefore, they excluded themselves from this celebration. Seventh Day Adventist's went to camp during the carnival season. I never missed the action though. I accompanied my grandmother or I snuck into the crowd. I was spiked with excitement as locals patrolled the streets wearing lively colors. The villagers crowded the streets which made it impossible to walk through them. People sat on the sidewalk and beat their drums and music filled the air. Men passed by in senseh costumes. Imagine wearing a senseh in ninety-degree weather. A senseh is a chicken with ruffled feathers. I remembered my Uncle Jake made a senseh using pieces of fabric material which were then sewed to a bag. Old school calypso music filled the air, songs like "Mary Mary Jumping Up," "Marry the Girl Charlie," and "Bernie Get Up Slowly. Those were my Uncle Jake's favorite songs. Everyone shook their backsides to the music. When I danced to those songs my grandmother yelled, "*Sorti la avec vieux woolma sal ou!* (Move away from there with your dirty dance). My grandmother hardly spoke English. My grandmother spoke French Creole especially when she was angry.

Savory aromas of food filled the air. One could smell the barbeque chicken off the grills of some of the vendors. Homemade cakes, coconut cheese, and tamarind balls were sold as well. I would give anything to have coconut cheese right now. I spent the money I had on snow cones and other items. The money in Dominica is of a different currency from that of the United States. The dollars were octagon shaped. Silver coins and one-dollar bills from the United States were equal to two dollars and seventy cents in Eastern Caribbean dollars.

I looked forward to Creole Day, a national day in Dominica. On this day, Dominicans spoke French Creole all day, a language also known as Patoi or Patwa On Creole Day, Dominicans dressed, danced, spoke, and ate Creole food. Weeks prior to Creole Day, my aunt went to town and bought the fabric material, lace, and ribbon for our traditional outfit. We had our own seamstress who took our measurements and we would be informed of when to retrieve it when it was finished. This seamstress also made my uniforms for school and any outfit I wanted which I cut out from magazines.

One Creole Day, my grandmother placed her pearls around my neck with matching earrings and applied makeup and lipstick to my face. A girl was never too young to adorn herself during festivals. My grandmother always made sure I looked as sophisticated as she was. I didn't have a full wob dwiyet (a long-decorated petticoat); however, I loved to see the women wear them at the Miss Wob Dwiyet competitions. I had on a jip, a white cotton blouse and a skirt trimmed with lace and red ribbon with matching headpiece. Couples danced the African form of traditional dance, Belé, while men beat on their tanbou (drums) on sidewalks. One man blew his flute as kids sang and danced. The songs played were traditional jing ping (Dominican folk music) as my friends and I danced the traditional folk dance. We danced heel and toe to the beat of the drums.

Later, I returned home to my Uncle Jake, filled with excitement over a bag of kwapo (crapaud) toads known as mountain chicken that he caught. What he boiled in the pot was not appetizing. They resembled white frogs. The craziest thing was that my uncle enjoyed the kwapo. What I devoured was a creole dish with codfish, breadfruit, and pelau (palow). Other traditional dishes were callaloo and sancoche. All these mouth-watering foods will have you returning for more. Speaking of returning, I wish to return to Dominica again one day.

Sadly, Dominica was the first island hit by the category five hurricane Maria on September 18th, 2017. Hurricane Maria crippled my country which was left to God's mercy. On Christmas 2017, people in my village were still waiting for electricity. What men took years to build was destroyed in a day which is why I am humble. This is year 2020, but tomorrow is not promised. I thank God for the lives of my family living in the islands.

# CHAPTER 3

# Middle School

*E*lementary schools in Dominica were from first to seventh grade. School started at nine in the morning and ended three-thirty in the afternoon. Students' arrival was expected before the bell rang for assembly as tardiness was inexcusable. My aunt taught me that the early bird catches the worm.

In Dominica, children wore uniforms to school with their natural hair. Elementary schools are remarkably different from schools in the United States.

My classroom had twenty-five children, mostly girls. I was too talkative to remember what I learned in school, still, I performed better than satisfactory. What we looked forward to the most was recess around noon. We spent recess outside and we played games such as hide and seek, hopscotch and a ball game called Monkey in the Middle. Boys and girls played a game called rounders, almost like soccer. Students loved me on their team since I was a fast runner. I was always ready for a challenge when it came to racing; however, I was no tomboy. I remembered a day I brought my Barbie doll to school to show to friends. I also sewed fabric out of worn-out clothing to make outfits for my dolls.

The best part of elementary school was the outdoor adventures the school called field trips as referred to Belle Maché in my country. On field trips, we took long walks to destinations out of the city. My cooler, which was filled with ice, turned to hot water by the end of the trip. On one field trip, I remembered I climbed Mount Diablotin (Devil's Mountain). That adventure took a whole day.

I remembered one year in elementary school the teacher arranged a Christmas party in class. In class we made Christmas cards out of poster cardboard and placed money in the cards. The cards were then distributed around the community to the less fortunate. Students were taught that Christmas was about giving rather than receiving and a little kindness went a long way. The world was unkind.

School was not always candy and rainbows for me. As a kid from eight to twelve years old, I was tall and thin. My aunt combed my thick, dark hair and added different color bubbles. These hairstyles called unwanted attention to me and as a result I got teased. I often chanted, "Sticks and stones may break my bones but words can do me no harm." Little did they know, words did great harm. My nicknames were decorated broomstick, spaghetti, and maga. I remembered a boy kicked my leg at school to see if it would break. Children also placed two fingers around my wrist to measure how skinny I was. I complained to my aunt however, and she would only say that she sent me to school to learn, not to fight.

At my aunt's house, we were huge wrestling fans. I anxiously waited for a Monday or Wednesday to watch Hulk Hogan, Sting, The Undertaker and The Rock. The Undertaker was my favorite. I loved the way they announced his arrival and how he buried his opponent after the fight. Wrestling was one of the things we watched together as a family; however, of all the wrestling I watched, I was defenseless at school when I was bullied. One day I was assaulted by a boy at school because I cheated in a race. The girl he liked, Bethany Abraham, was in front of me during the race and I pulled her to the back. I had too much pride to allow a fat girl to run faster than me. I also lifted Bethany's white, pleated skirt at an assembly and revealed her polka dot underwear for the school to see. Okay maybe this time I deserved to have gotten beaten up. I returned home beaten up and my grandmother rubbed my body with snake oil and made me a drink called Wemed Blessed (blessed remedy). My grandmother claimed that this disgusting drink with raw eggs would make me strong. I neglected to drink the remedy, but probably I should have.

I stopped being harassed when I learned to defend myself. My Uncle Jake's girlfriend, Deborah Leblanc told me that children would refrain from bullying me when I learned to defend myself. So I defended myself at school, and when I returned home, I was disciplined. Discipline was not being grounded like children in the United States. Discipline meant a beating. The school staff's form of punishment for students was to write, "I must behave myself in class" thousands of times on papers. Another form of punishment would be to get hit on the palm of your hands with an iron ruler. What soothed my soul was music.

Music was also an important part of my life growing up. I recall a few memories based on songs I had heard. The song Imagine by John Lennon puts a cloud over my head every time I hear it. Why? I was in the fifth grade in elementary school when a house burned down with a dog in it near the school. The air was filled with smoke as ashes floated around. When the ambulance arrived that day, imagine was playing inside the ambulance. That day was dark and cold, although the sky was sunny and bright. I believe the children's' mother forgot something on the stove when she went out, leaving the kids and a dog behind. I also remembered a boy at the age of seven who was the only survivor of a plane crash. It was a Cardinal flight coming in from Saint Martin. When the plane shook, bodies flew on top of the boy which shielded him from harm. The boy had a fifty percent chance of surviving but died in the ambulance. On the way to the hospital, the ambulance shook what was left of his organs. Imagine the story the boy would have shared if he had survived the crash. I forgot the name of the song that played when the news was announced, but songs can have an impact on a person. Songs can bring bad memories or good memories. At my aunt's wedding, I remember the song Endless Love and These Arms sung by All-4-One. My cousins and I were supposed to sing the song at my aunt's wedding; however, we got nervous when we saw the size of the crowd. Music has always been a part of my life at church or at school. I was in the Pathfinders group at church, though I never sang a solo. I sang soprano in the choir at school. The choir director taught us the songs Mocking Bird Hill, Music Moves Me, and Shalom Chaverim. These are the songs I can remember. At home I listened to gospel music by CeCe Winans, Yolanda Adams, and Kirk Franklin. My aunt was not interested in the upbeat gospel.

My aunt was intelligent and guided me throughout my years of school. She made sure I was more than satisfactory and followed the smarter students. My best friend was a girl who skipped from the fifth grade to seventh grade. My best friend is now a doctor in China. I imagined I would be happy when my aunt was my teacher in seventh grade; I was wrong. My aunt expected more from me, and when I failed to perform my best, I was taught, "spare the rod, spoil the child."

CHAPTER 4

# Spare the Rod, Spoil the Child

$I$n Dominica, corporal punishment was often used as parents believed their children were being disciplined. Parents were unaware they were being physically abusive.

The Biblical explanation my aunt gave for her disciplines was a phrase she got from the Bible called, spare the rod, spoil the child. It was taken from the book of Proverbs. I could not argue with the Bible, for the Bible came with spiritual instructions.

My aunt was my teacher when I was twelve in the seventh grade. My aunt was loved by many students and those students showed their appreciation on Teachers' Appreciation Day. I was always excited to help my aunt open gifts but not too thrilled about being in her class. My class consisted of approximately twenty-five students. I tried my best in class; however, the subject mathematics beat me up academically. My aunt disciplined me for my failure. I recalled being beaten with a leather belt as I ran under the table in the classroom to hide from her. My aunt moved the table and beat me with the belt. My aunt could not grasp the fact that other children in the classroom understood the math equations but I did not. The beatings did not improve my grade, but instead only led me to resent the subject. Students sympathized with me but were unable to help. I fought back once in class when my aunt attempted to hit me with the leather belt. When my aunt swung the belt I caught the belt and hit her with it.

I am the oldest of my father's five children. I had two other siblings, Zelda and Junior before my father remarried. My siblings usually visited Dominica during the summer. The summer was splendid until my siblings did something wrong. I often was punished for my siblings misbehavior because I was the oldest. My sister was eight and my brother was around two years old. My little brother dared not urinate in bed. One day I overheard my aunt on the phone with my grandmother. My aunt said, "Ma, Junior peed in bed again." My grandmother came from home and beat my little brother. She beat him with a coconut broom made out of long, thin sticks. My little brother's bedwetting was uncontrollable and he kept getting beaten. That particular summer with my siblings was short since my siblings mother called to mention that they were going to Disneyland. That was the last time I saw my brother and sister.

❧

Boys were forbidden.

"Talking to boys will get you pregnant, and when that happens, don't bother to come home!" That was my grandmother's harsh way of educating me about boys. One day I sat on the stairs of my aunt's house and spoke to my cousin Andrew. My Uncle Alfred saw me and reported to my aunt that he saw me speaking to a boy outside. Yes, I got my ass whooped, slapped, and punched with no questions asked.

My curfew was when the sun set at six in the evening. I had to be home before then. One evening I lost track of time at one of my friend's house and missed curfew. My friend's older brother,

Austin, walked me home to ensure my safety. My Uncle Jake saw me walking with Austin and I knew he would have told my aunt. My aunt had a belt waiting for me upon arrival. As soon as I stepped into the house, she leashed her wrath upon me. Boys withdrew from me just to spare me the beatings. When my aunt grew weary of beating on me, she asked my grandmother to hit me. My grandmother asked my Uncle Alfred when she got tired.

One Saturday afternoon, I forgot what I did wrong. I only remember the day was a Saturday since my grandmother spoke of attending church the following day. That Saturday I stood in the shower and my grandmother walked heavily to the bathroom. My grandmother picked up a basin and hit me on the head repeatedly. The basin fell to the floor then she used her fist. I remember my cousin Sophia telling me that they kept hitting me since I refused to fight back. I took a flexible clip from my hair and stabbed my grandmother numerous times in the chest. My act of insanity scared the hell out of her. My grandmother avoided service the following Sunday. My grandmother and my aunt asked my Uncle Alfred to hit me since they were afraid to raise their hands to me.

One day my Uncle Alfred was about to beat me but I had an evil smile on my face. I noticed my uncle had a carbuncle under his arm. I hurried to his bar and picked up an icepick then threatened to burst his carbuncle if he touched me. I became so bad my aunt said I should see the priest because I had the devil in me. I was not bad, just exhausted from getting hurt for unjust reasons.

I had a tall, thin, light skinned friend named Emma in my classroom. One day Emma stole a quarter from her mother's purse. As punishment, Emma's mother placed her hand in a pot of boiling water. Olivia, the other friend I hung out with said that Emma often came to her house to play. Emma showed Olivia and her mother her hand and they were saddened with grief. Emma's epidermis was removed and her fingers were burnt. Olivia told me that the skin on her hand was discolored.

Emma later left her mother's house and went to live with her grandmother. Emma's mother never served time in prison. My friend Olivia left Dominica at the age of eleven.

In the United States, corporal punishment is rarely used; however, in Dominica discipline was abuse. On March 31st, 2016, a newspaper article announced that corporal punishment remained legal though educational officials demanded alternative methods of discipline.

The Education Act stated that corporal punishment should be used as last resort as many other strategies could be used to discipline children.

I over studied for the common entrance exam yet I still failed it. The common entrance exam was an exam students took to transition to high school. I expressed how I felt with my first poem at the age of twelve. The poem went like this:

*I failed my exam and was not glad I didn't even tell my Dad*
*think this is bad, I should have been mad.*

I wanted to attend the Isaiah Thomas Secondary School since all my friends were attending there in September. I begged my aunt to avoid sending me to high school in Salisbury for I disliked the green uniform. Thankfully, my aunt spoke of a school in another district I could attend. I was pleased to learn that my cousin Sophia and two friends of mine were going to the same school that September.

The school looked great on the outside and so did the students in their uniforms. What you failed to see was what happened on the inside. The difference between this high school and the other high schools was that at this high school, one had to learn to survive.

# CHAPTER 5

# Surviving High School

What was high school like? I would compare my experience of high school to the movie Matilda that starred by Danny DeVito, Mara Wilson and Pam Ferris as Ms. Trunchbull. I was Matilda, the girl who looked forward to school and my principal, Ma George, was like Ms. Trunchbull who darkened the school days.

The Greenville Secondary School surrounded a large playfield. The school was painted blue and white like the colors of our uniform. The girls wore navy blue pleated skirts with white button-down shirts, navy blue socks, and black shoes. The boys wore navy blue long pants with white button-down shirts. Both boys and girls complemented the school uniform with a navy blue tie which had the school's symbol.

In Dominica, secondary schools ranged from first to fifth forms rather than eighth to twelve grade. Every day I rode the public bus to and from school. School started at eight in the morning and ended at two-thirty. On the first day, of school I was relieved to see my cousin Sophia along with friends from my village.

The principal conducted assembly before school started. During assembly we stood outside in lines and sang songs of psalms and read Bible scriptures. I felt as though I was at a Pentecostal church. Students walked to class after assembly. The subjects we studied in class were general studies. The subjects we studied included English, French, geography, history, literature, mathematics, principles of business, science and social Studies. English and literature were my favorite subjects since I loved writing essays and short stories. Mathematics was a challenge for me in both elementary and secondary school. The only thing I remembered about history was Napoleon Bonaparte, the French statesman, and Amerigo Vespucci. My friends and I made fun of the names. We uttered Napoleon Boda Plat and Amerigo Vespussy. Although funny at the time, I should have taken my education seriously.

The principal wanted to invest strong moral and spiritual values into us students so she made her own subject. The principal called this subject Moral and Spiritual Instructions. Students were taught the Bible. The principal stated that in order to transfer to the next class, we had to pass her subject. I felt sympathy toward the students who were not raised in a religious household. I studied my Bible like a regular textbook which pleased my aunt.

I had a crush on my geography teacher who my friend Meggan called "Sir Sparks." I am sure every girl has had a schoolgirl crush. What did I like about him? Maybe it was his intelligence and boyish looks. The teachers at the school were very young, like they had completed college only recently. Meggan often teased me about Sir Sparks. Most of my punishment at school could have been avoided if I did not follow Meggan and Sophia. Meggan was a short, plump, light-skinned girl who loved to laugh. Meggan was the class clown and though one may not find her jokes to be funny, her laughter was the joke. Meggan snorted at the end of her laugh which I found hilarious. I loved to laugh as well which got me into trouble. When my friends and I disrupted the class, we did not get the "chokey," we got spanked by the principal or worse.

Not only had I endured abuse at home, but school was no consolation. The math teacher escorted Sophia and I out of class one day and we were sent to the principal's office for disruptive behavior. The principal commanded Sophia and I to kneel in the middle of the school field with both of our hands raised in the air. The principal commanded us to hold a heavy, large rock in each hand. Students walking by giggled at the sight. My cousin and I resembled statues on the school field. We remained in that position for the entire class period and missed recess. The principal spied on us to ensure we remained in the position. Sophia and I placed our tired hands down when the principal was not looking. I mentally traveled to another place as time progressed. I ignored the brutal sun which beamed down on me in the humidity. I felt as though I was inhaling heat from an oven and was anxious to return to class.

In class, my name was popular because I was one of five Aishas. The Aishas were all special in their own way, but I was the talkative one. One of the Aishas was called "man framed" and my nickname was "Crazo." Sir Sparks teased me since he stated I resembled Angelica in the Rugrats due to my hairstyle. One day, I stood in front of assembly to apologize to Sir Sparks. I forgot the reason; however, I was filled with embarrassment. A spanking would have been acceptable for me at that moment. Speaking of spanking, male teachers often spanked female students on the bottom and the principal continued her unreasonable punishments. About eleven students proceeded with their complaints to the Board of Education; however, the issue remained unresolved. The Board of Education stated that they needed more students to come forward. My friends and I did not complain, we probably should have. Students sang, "be bold, be strong" in assembly, but the principal stood strong.

Tardy students who arrived at school after assembly were given a machete to cut grass on the field. I remembered I skipped breakfast some mornings to avoid tardiness, but I arrived late and had to cut grass in the blazing sun anyway. The principal had brought back slavery, my friend Meggan said once she arrived late to school and a teacher made her run around the large field. Imagine a chubby girl running around a large field in blazing heat. In Dominica we have no seasons—we have summer all year. Dominicans suffer unbearable heat. One day, a teacher commanded me to stand for a long period of time in the middle of the field and I fainted. One of the students pushed a lollipop in my mouth to revive me. I refrained from complaining to My aunt since my aunt thought the principal was doing a wonderful job with the school.

On Fridays, I often pretended to be sick to be absent from school. One Friday, my friends and I decided to go on strike and we stayed at the bus stop. I felt that school on Fridays was a waste of time. I had two subjects on Fridays, physical education and mathematics. A few students complained that the male teachers looked under their skirts when they bent down. On Fridays, we wore a different uniform. Students had teams and wore different colored t-shirts according to their team color and white pleated skirts. I was on the red team and competed in certain challenges in sports. I remembered competing in a bag race. Students placed their legs inside of a bag and tried to jump. Boys did labor with cement and bricks, work that hired employees should have done. I was glad I was not a boy to do hard labor. If I attended school on Fridays, I wore my red, short tights with faux diamonds on the sides under my white skirt. We had no gym for physical education, we performed hard labor or engaged in sports outside.

School was not always dark. The valuable memories I have of high school were of socializing with friends and singing in the choir. During lunch break, my friends and I socialized under a tree which provided shade. We shared food among ourselves, eavesdropped on older students, discussed who were still a virgin, and sang songs. We sang songs by Shaba ranks and Buju Banton. My friends and I loved to sing.

The principal had two daughters who taught at the school. One teacher taught principles of business and the other daughter was a choir instructor at the school. The songs the choir director chose had great meaning for they conveyed a message. I remembered three songs our school choir sang. We sang I Have a Dream by Robert Buiten Kamp, Future Generation by 4 HIM, and Destined to Win, a song by Reverend Jessy Dixon. My favorite song was Future Generation. I wanted to be the lead singer and sing a solo, but a girl with a powerful voice was chosen for the lead instead. I loved the words of the song for it started, *I won't bend and I won't break*. We competed against other schools and performed extremely well. I remembered once we won third place and Salisbury School won first place. Salisbury School sang One Moment in Time. My grandmother pressed my uniform with extra love, ironing gracefully pleat by pleat. Those were the experiences I enjoyed.

My class raised money for a limousine a few semesters before graduation. One student collected money from us weekly as we placed any amount we had in a jar. My friends and I discussed hairstyles we wanted and high heeled shoes we would wear with our graduation gown. I contemplated singing Forever Friends for "Breakup Day." Breakup Day was the last day of school where students signed each other's uniform shirts with autographs.

In our last semester of school, the principal broke our spirits when she uttered that only one child would graduate. We worked so hard throughout the years even though students like me were irksome. The principal stated only one child, Lucille Adams, would graduate. Although I was teased for being thin, Lucille looked like a skeleton compared to me covered in dark skin. However, how she looked did not prevent her from giving the best academic performance in class. Lucille Adams was a straight A student. Once she got a B on a test and she cried as though she got hurt. Lucille was afraid to return home from school that day. Lucille's family had high expectations for her.

The principal boasted she would throw a surprise dinner for Lucille and her family. What about the rest of the class? As proud and elated as Lucille was, she was saddened by the fact that her classmates would not walk down the aisle with her to get their diplomas. The principal made known that our diplomas would be mailed to us. We were crushed. In a class of twenty-five children, one child was selected to graduate.

On the last day of school, we signed each other's uniforms and yearbooks. We did not get the limousine we wanted but we did have fun throwing rocks at the school from a truck. I heard some students were getting together at a beach after and I wanted to go. I wanted to accompany my friends, but my aunt refused to give me permission to leave the house. That day was the last day I saw my classmates, but I did continue to see my cousin and friends who lived in my village. Years went by and some of my classmates and my cousin remained friends on Facebook. My wish is that we all could get reunited one day and get dressed in the graduation gowns that were denied to us. We would graduate and walk down the aisle and our proud family would watch us as we accept our diplomas. The school closed years later. There have been reports on an investigation into the practices and procedures of that Christian school.

As adults we go to work and force a smile, though we often have emotional baggage. We are told to leave our problems at home before attending work. While my friends and I attended high school, we had problems we left at home. What has happened behind closed doors I have forgiven, yet I have not forgotten.

## CHAPTER 6

# Forgiven But Not Forgotten

I lived with my Aunt Eleanor and her husband Steve in a three-bedroom house. The rooms and bathroom were upstairs and the kitchen and living room were downstairs. Steve worked as a prison guard and my aunt was a teacher at the Saint Joseph Elementary School. As for me, I was still trying to survive high school.

I returned home from school around three to three thirty since I took the bus home. My aunt returned from school around five o'clock. My aunt stayed at school to grade children's papers, distribute report cards or for a meeting. Steve reached home after I did and we fought over the television. Steve took the remote from my hand to change the channel to watch sports or news. I enjoyed watching Punky Brewster, Kids Songs, or Captain Planet. When Steve took over the television I had no choice but to walk upstairs to my room. Steve always looked at me when I walked up the stairs. One day Steve said that he saw my underwear, smiled, and revealed what color underwear I wore. The love seat was located near the window and the large sofa where he sat was placed near the stairs. I dismissed Steve's perversion and became more conservative. I wore short tights under my skirts or I ran up the stairs when he was there.

I sat to watch television one day after school. Steve arrived but neglected to take the remote from my hand this time. Steve passed his hand up my leg. I was startled and shook my leg. Steve made a comment about the hair on my leg. Wasn't I supposed to have hair on my legs? As a woman, I use Nair to remove unwanted hairs on my body. But at fourteen years old, I was unaware of what was acceptable. Steve tried to educate me about being a woman. A topic I was not prepared for. I remembered I saw the word "Sex" written on the bathroom wall at school. One day I asked my aunt what sex meant.

My aunt replied, "Aisha, read a book."

My grandmother taught me that boys plus books equals belly. I also read books with educational poems that I loved.

We seemed like the perfect family at church, but no one knew what lurked behind closed doors.

One morning my aunt and Steve were home. My aunt sent me upstairs to help Steve with something. I forgot what I had to help Steve with, but we had to go to the bank after. I entered the room and Steve who had a towel cloaked around him, unwrapped the towel. Steve showed me his private parts. I threatened to tell my aunt and headed towards the stairs. Steve rushed to his green uniform pants which hung on the room door, took the black belt from the pants and pointed the belt buckle to my face. Steve grabbed me and threatened to hit me with the belt if I uttered a word to my aunt.

The following day I spoke to Deborah, my Uncle Jake's girlfriend, about what happened in the house. Deborah was not surprised when I told her about Steve.

Deborah uttered, " He's probably just like his brother. He has a brother that is sick in his head, he shows his penis to the kids near the bridge up the river." Deborah suggested I should tell my aunt.

I was unsure of how to approach my aunt so I told my grand-mother. My grandmother bore everyone's burden. Every day my grandmother gave me a picnic basket with containers of food to distribute to the family. Food was distributed to my two uncles, Alfred and Jake. Uncle Jake's six- and seven-year-old girls got food and my aunt, her husband, and I got food. When I informed my grandmother about Steve that day, she withheld food from him. Later I spoke to my aunt about her husband and she was furious.

My aunt shouted, "You just want to destroy my marriage of seven years. You can't stand to see me happy!"

I cried, "Auntie you have to believe me."

My aunt yelled, "Why should I believe you? You're good at making up stories!"

My aunt stated that I told lies in my diary and she would burn it. My aunt refrained from using profanity; however, she called me a pig and a crab. My aunt was infuriated, breathing heavily and quickened her steps when she walked. An awkward silence filled the house after we argued that day. No one in the house exchanged words. What was left was a twenty-dollar bill on the table every week. The twenty-dollar bill was money to buy lunch at school every week. Sometimes I avoided the money or refused to eat. I felt like a picture on the wall. Everyone knew I was there, yet no one acknowledged me. Tension grew in the house and my aunt thought anything could be fixed with prayer.

My aunt and her husband fought like any other couple. One day I intervened in their fight and regretted that decision. Steve took the dirty mop which stood on the side of the fridge and mopped my face with it. I learned to mind my business and not interfere when they fought. In Dominica, domestic issues are resolved in the home. No one calls the police about any distur-bances. What happens in the house stays in the house.

I had cruel intentions at home. I recalled leaving the room door slightly open. I had a knife placed under my pillow. The plan was to cut Steve if he tried to hurt me. Steve had a younger

brother who was infatuated with me. One day Steve gave me letters and said they were from his brother. One of the letters had
a drawing of a nude man and woman in a heart. I giggled child-
ishly at the sight of it. I spoke to my cousin Sophia about the letters I received. Sophia uttered that Steve must have written the
letters. I compared the letter to a Christmas card Steve signed to
confirm. The handwriting in the letter was similar to the writing
on the card. I was shocked. I remembered all the things written
in the letter, the condoms, and the ring Steve kicked under my
door.

One rainy night I allowed my kitten to sleep in the house.
The kitten urinated and moved its bowels in the kitchen. In the
morning, I heard Steve yell about killing my kitten. I ran down
the stairs. Steve looked at me as he held my kitten by the neck
and broke its neck. My heart sank. Words could not express how
I felt.

I confided in my cousin Sophia. Sophia and I got into mischief
at school and got punished together. Sophia's mother always
played music by Patsy Cline or Skeeter Davis. I remembered the
song, 'Face of a Clown' which played in the background. The
words of the song was how I felt. Songs do bring back memories.

Sophia was upset when I informed her of what happened at
my home. Sophia stated she would put voodoo (witchcraft) on
Steve allowing him to become sick. Sophia added that no doctors
would know the cause of Steve's illness. Sophia made known of
a list of things she needed that belonged to Steve. Sophia stated
she needed: three toenails, three fingernails, and three strands of
hair from Steve's head. I was angry at Steve and curious; however, I forbid Sophia from going through with anything. When
you do bad to people, bad comes back to you three times worse.
Sadly, witchcraft is practiced in Dominica. I saw a girl run naked
on the street one day. The girl shed clothes as if bugs crawled
on her. The girl's friend's grandmother placed witchcraft on the
girl out of jealousy. I stood with a huge crowd at the back of my
aunt's house. I heard different voices expelled out of the girl's

mouth. I heard babies crying and a man's voice. A priest had come and exorcised twelve demon spirits out of the girl.

I explained to Sophia that if Steve is the person my aunt wants in her life, I want no part of it. I said I would ask my father to send for me from Saint Thomas. My father was not pleased when I spoke to him. I was present when my aunt and father spoke on the phone. My aunt spoke of my poor performance at school. My father responded he would send for me and I could continue my education in Saint Thomas. My aunt suggested that my father should wait until I graduated from high school to send for me since I had one year left.

We had a new addition to the home in 1997. My aunt had her own daughter who was a bundle of joy. I completed high school years later. I chanted, "No more pencils, no more books, no more teachers dirty looks." In the summer of 2000, I left Dominica to live with my father, stepmother, and little sister in Saint Thomas.

In the year 2017, I befriended Steve on social media. I forgave Steve, not for him, but for me. The heaviness lifted off my shoulders. Sophia and I were friends on Facebook. I asked Sophia if she remembered our conversation when I was a teenager and her response.

Sophia said, "Yes I was so pissed when you told me. I wanted to kill him. I was mad at your aunt for not seeing what kind of person he was, blinded by love."

My aunt said in 1996 she would burn my diary. In November of 2017 my aunt confessed that she has my diary. My aunt has kept my diary for twenty-four years awaiting my return to Dominica.

# CHAPTER 7

# Saint Thomas

I left Dominica and embarked on a journey to Saint Thomas in the summer of 2000. I had traveled with my family on summer vacations before; however, I traveled alone that day.

I sat on the plane and was lost in my thoughts. I wondered where the urine went when someone went to the restroom of a plane. Did the urine get absorbed into the clouds? I thought too much. I imagined Saint Thomas would bring me joy. Many Dominicans longed to migrate to the United States in hopes of a better life. I was fortunate to have the opportunity. I was excited I was going to live with my father, stepmother, and my five-year-old sister. My stepmother was a kind, young woman. I was about twelve years old when my father married this woman. This woman, my stepmother, was old enough to be my big sister. My family tolerated my stepmother, though they assumed she was a gold digger. I liked my stepmother for she reminded my father he had a daughter named Aisha. I heard that my father's first wife was cruel. My father made a remark of her being psychologically damaged. My father's first wife saw her mother jump from a building when she was a young child. I assumed this experience would have a negative impact on an individual.

My family drove me home from the airport when I arrived in Saint Thomas. My family lived in a town called Annas Retreat. The place was warm and inviting in a peaceful environment. Trees in the area provided shade though attracted mosquitoes. I was extremely bored at home. Boredom bothered me more than mosquitoes. I was so bored I watched soap operas in Spanish. My father seldom watched television. My father worked as a security guard at the Ramada Inn Hotel and always kept occupied.

My stepmother worked at the Caribbean Rumballs Factory. My sister and I accompanied my stepmother to work in the morning. My stepmother worked in a pleasant environment where she joked and socialized with co-workers. One of the coworkers was her friend from Dominica. I helped my stepmother roll the rum-soaked balls at the factory. The rum balls were to be rolled and packed in small boxes to be sent to cruise ships.

At home I played music, talked to my father's parrot, or I went to the mall. The Havensight Mall in Saint Thomas should be called Heavensight. I spent most of my time at this mall. My stepmother believed the mall was my second home. I loved the attractions from gifts, souvenirs, jewelry, and more. I went to the beach or took a walk in the neighborhood when I was not at the mall. I relaxed on the weekends. My father wanted me to continue to attend church on Saturdays. He sent me to an Adventist church with an elderly woman. I remembered one Saturday a Haitian boy sang a solo in church. The boy sang When I'm Crying Jesus in French Creole.

August 28th was my eighteenth birthday. My stepmother organized a party at Coki Beach near Red Hook for me. Few friends I attended elementary school with were present, but there were many strangers. My stepmother arose early to cook that day. She cooked a variety of food, enough to feed an entire community. My father jokingly commented that she conducted the party for Saint Thomas rather than for me.

My stepmother was a compassionate soul; however, I wondered what my biological mother was like. Did my mother love to laugh like me? Was my mother sophisticated? I wondered if I resembled my mother as I differed from my father. My father had Carib, curly hair like my grandmother. My siblings resembled my father.

When I was fourteen years old I received a letter from my mother. My mother stated that she wrote and sent me letters often. My mother presumed she mailed the letters to the Dominican Republic. I replied to my mother with a letter and photo of me. I wore a blue, sleeveless top with matching pants as I sat on a white wicker chair. I accused my aunt of withholding letters from me.. My aunt reminded me of how my mother abandoned me. That was the last and only letter I received from my mother.

I asked my father about my mother. My father yelled in an aggravated tone of voice, "Why are you asking about your mother now? Your mother never called; she does not care about you!"

My father made known that my aunt was my mother. My father mentioned I had a brother in Saint Thomas and would take me to visit him.

One Sunday afternoon, my father took me to visit my brother. My brother Kyle lived with his aunt and four children in a wooden house on top of a hill. The house was remarkably fragile, tilted on one side. It appeared that if a person stepped too hard, the house would lean over and fall. My brother explained that hurricane Marilyn was the cause of the house's poor appearance. Kyle attended the Reserved Officers Training Corps (ROTC) program. My Aunt Catherine has four children, three girls and one boy. My Aunt Catherine, my mother's older sister, raised Kyle after his father passed away. My aunt took me to Kmart, Marianne's and the TuTu Park Mall to shop for clothing. My brother spoke of how my mother longed to see me and that she never stopped looking for me. At the end of the day, my brother and I exchanged phone numbers and I returned home.

My father approached me as I sat on the couch one day. My father said that I needed an education and I explained I finished high school. My father continued saying that I needed to get a job. My father took me to apply at McDonald's restaurant the following day.

My father drove me to work at McDonald's restaurant every morning. I felt a sense of independence working at this fast-paced job. The job paid five dollars and fifty cents an hour. I worked as a crew member in the kitchen. I prepared food, cleaned, and served customers. The manager, Lenard, favored a man called Speedy. Speedy was a fast worker who could make many burgers in one minute. I indulged myself in apple pies and nuggets when no one looked. I later regretted that decision when I returned home to a fat and greasy face.

One hot afternoon, my stepmother and I had an argument. My stepmother shouted, "You just came to Saint Thomas and you're already talking to a man on the phone!"

The only friend I had in Saint Thomas was a man I was for-bidden to see. I spoke to my brother on the phone most of the time. I argued with my stepmother. I fumed with rage only to be stopped by a slap across my face. My father laid his hand on me for the first time. I was indecisive of what was worse, my father's slap or his stuttering. I told my father to notify me when he could speak. I felt embarrassed for my father as he struggled to speak.

The following day my father told me that I could not work at McDonald's all my life. My father explained that I needed a career and an education. My father added that he did not need two women in his house. My father tried to enroll me at the University of the Virgin Islands (UVI), but I failed the written exam. I was also informed I had a foreign diploma. The plan to attend college was unsuccessful. My father tried to enroll me in the navy. I failed the navy's test and felt discouraged. My father seemed determined and spoke of the army. My father and I both agreed I was unprepared for the army. I saw army boot camp on television. A person had to be mentally and physically prepared to join the army.

October 4th, 2000, I filled out an application to enroll at the Delaware Valley Job Corps.. The counselor in admissions interviewed me. A test was unnecessary for acceptance at the Job Corps Center. I just needed my name on the list. My father and I were told that the place was in a cold climate. We were oblivious as to what cold meant. The only place my father and I knew was cold was inside of a refrigerator. Saint Thomas is a tropical Island; it's summer all year round.

I resigned at McDonald's and gave the manager two weeks' notice. I mentioned I needed to further my education. My father believed I was unproductive with my time, although I did work. My father said I would obtain my GED and trade of my choice and then qualify for a good profession and salary. My father had good intentions; however, I felt like a misbehaved child being sent away to boarding school. I felt as though my father was determined to get rid of me.

October 30th, 2000, I wore a pleather (plastic leather) jacket, black tights, and tall boots to go on the trip to the job corps. If you asked me, I resembled Puss in Boots. What my father was unaware of was that I was entering a whole new world.

# CHAPTER 8

## *A Whole New World*

*O*n October 30th, 2000, my family drove me to the airport. I had no idea my life was about to change. I met a girl named Lisa at the airport. Lisa spoke of her boyfriend at the Delaware Valley Job Corps. Lisa looked at my attire and warned that the weather was below freezing at the center. She gave me extra layers of clothing from her suitcase. My pleather jacket, black tights and boots were unsuitable for the cold climate.

We arrived at the center late at midnight. The center looked haunted with the gate surrounding the building. The bitter, frigid air threatened to numb my exposed skin. I was pleased to have the extra clothing. Lisa and I were escorted to the female dormitory where I shared a room with three other roommates. My roommates were Gloria, Sheila, and Chelsey. My roommates showed me my locker and went to bed.

I saw the beauty of the center in the morning. The center had a stunning view of the Delaware Valley River. A place student's called "Little Puerto Rico" caught my interest. I have never been to Puerto Rico; however, I could imagine how beautiful Puerto Rico must be.

Job Corps is a self-paced program and I had set a goal to complete the program within a year. I needed six months to complete my trade and six months to complete my GED diploma.

A resident advisor, Miss Lala, was my alarm clock in the morning. Miss Lala knocked on everyone's room door singing, "Brunch, Brunch, Brunch!" Miss Lala was annoyingly funny; however, if we missed brunch we would have been extremely hungry.

The line to the cafeteria included students from both male and female dormitories. I lost my appetite when the time approached to place food on my plate. I was unaccustomed to American food. I ate an apple and drank apple juice from a soda fountain.

The cafeteria was packed with students and everyone seemed to be in groups of a variety of colors. I later found out that the crew who wore yellow called themselves "Latin Kings." Students who identified themselves as "Bloods" wore red and "Crips" wore blue attire. The rest of the students were from New York and the Virgin Islands. I was unable to connect with the students from the Virgin Islands, though I was from the Virgin Islands. The students said I spoke funny. I sat alone at a table in the cafeteria. On my way to class, a student on top of the stairs spat into my hair. I ran upstairs to the nearest restroom to wash it out. Gross! I realized the students needed to learn more than academics to prepare for their careers. Students needed proper manners. I disliked the center; I did not belong there. The gates around the center made me feel trapped and barricaded. I was locked from the outside world like being in a prison. I completed high school and had a job. I felt angry at my father for sending me to the Job Corps, yet I wanted to make him proud. I decided to "tough it out."

I noticed odd behavior, such as a girl kissing another girl near the gazebo. That was the first time I saw women kiss. I minded my business or tried to. Everyone had their cliques which limited my chances at making friends. I almost got assaulted one day for wearing red. A boy asked if I was a Blood. I was not part of any crew; red was just my favorite color.

On November 13th, 2000, I started learning the trade, hotel business clerk. My instructor was Mr. Carl Dailey, a man who loved poetry. I saw that he wrote a poem on his computer in class.

This trade offered many great opportunities. I could work as a reservationist at a hotel, be a travel attendant, or work at an airport.

One day in Mr. Dailey's class, a girl named Nancy pulled my book from my hand while I was writing a poem. Nancy read my poem aloud to the class. I was embarrassed but noticed her reaction. I noticed a tiny blush on Nancy's light-skinned, fat cheek as she read my poem. I could tell Nancy enjoyed my poem. No sense in complaining, my high-pitched voice was drowned by the students in the class. Students said I had a weird accent, while others mimicked me when I spoke. I felt cold and secluded in this new world.

The best experience I had was when I saw snow for the first time in the winter. I ran outside to join the other students.

A boy yelled, "It's the first time the V.I.'s see snow!"

Everyone from the Virgin Islands, Saint Croix, and Saint Thomas explored the snow. We played like little children in the snow. I stuck my tongue out and watched the snow fall and melt on my tongue. The only place I had seen snow was on the television. I called my aunt in Dominica to report how cold the climate was. I described the cold to her as being in a fridge. My aunt mentioned how hot Dominica was and I joked about sending her some snow. I described snow as frost in a freezer. The experience was memorable.

On December 12th, 2000, my counselor, Miss Williams, referred me to a therapist, Dr. Bill Smith. I was referred because I had difficulty adjusting to the Job Corps Center. Dr. Smith became the only confidant I could express my feelings to. I informed him I had never been away from the Virgin Islands before and felt homesick. Dr. Smith agreed to meet with me regularly. According to my file, I made an appointment to meet with Dr. Smith after winter break.

December 20th, 2000 began winter break. I had the option of going to New York or Saint Thomas. I chose to have my winter break in Saint Thomas since I missed the warm climate.

I spent many days in the sun in Saint Thomas and visited my old co-workers at McDonalds. My supervisor, Lennard, asked if I wanted to return to work and I accepted the offer. He was grateful he did not have to train me.

I loved being home; however, I had to return to the center in January. I misplaced my plane ticket the day I was supposed to return to the Job Corps Center. My father was infuriated with me. My father assumed I got rid of the ticket on purpose to remain in Saint Thomas. My father called the Job Corps Center to notify them of the lost ticket. I was surprised when I received another plane ticket right away. I returned to the center unaware of what awaited me. That day was the last day I saw my family. I was eighteen years old.

I regretted traveling to Saint Thomas for the winter break. The trip was like traveling from the oven to the fridge. I should have gone to New York to become better adjusted to the cold climate. To make matters worse, I had no scarf or warm coat. On January 16th and 17th, I was sick with the flu and had a fever of 102.2. I visited my favorite nurse Debby who mentioned I had bronchitis and sinusitis on the 29th of January. I continued to meet with Dr. Bill Smith weekly unless I was sick, which was often.

In February 2001, I still struggled with mathematics and failed the GED test. I was the most hated person in math class. I felt the math teacher's resentment towards me. The math teacher, Miss Berns, brought her daughter to school one day and Nancy lied to Miss Berns. Nancy told Miss Berns that I showed her daughter the middle finger. Miss Berns pulled her daughter closer to her as she believed this false accusation. If looks could kill, I would be dead.. The entire class looked at me with disgust. Students yelled at me, and Nancy hid her evil smile. I was humiliated, angry, and sick of being the victim.

I wanted to avoid Miss Berns class. The students constantly disrupted it. One student, Jeff, asked me where I was from. I responded I was from the Virgin Islands, though I was raised in a different country. Jeff was from New York; therefore, I stated I had some family in Brooklyn. A girl interrupted the conversation and said that people from the Bronx disliked people from Brooklyn. A few students shouted, "B.X in the house!" I turned around to face the front of the class and felt a crumbled paper hit me at the back of my head. A student, Jasmine Deary, threw pencils at me. I addressed the issue to the teacher; however, Miss Berns ignored me and kept writing math solutions on the board. Infuriated I was being ignored, I sharpened one of the pencils Jasmine threw at me. I rose from my seat and walked over to where Jasmine sat. I grabbed Jasmine's palm and stabbed her with the pointed pencil. I felt no remorse. Jasmine complained to Miss Berns and Miss Berns gave me a demerit, but then changed her mind. Miss Berns decided that the incident was assault and I should report to the CEO office. Jasmine walked around the classroom and showed the students what I did to her hand. All of a sudden Jasmine was the victim.

I sat on the floor near the CEO, Mr. Marks, office and contemplated on how to plead my case. I was apathetic about getting terminated. Jeff and Jasmine pointed at me and laughed as they walked in my direction. Jasmine confessed she largened the hole and showed me the palm of her hand. In Mr. Marks office, I spoke of what happened in class. Mr. Marks said that since this was my first offense, I would do hundreds of hours of community service in the cafeteria.

I spoke to Dr. Smith after school and explained I was provoked. I cleaned the tables in the cafeteria, washed the dishes, and threw out the trash. The students passed their dirty, plastic dishes to be cleaned or place them on the counter. A boy spit in his plate before he gave it to me. I handled community service well since I had two Haitian girls there to help me. They spoke French Creole as I did and I wished they were my roommates.

I got along with my roommates Gloria, Chelsey, and Sheila and loved their Jamaican accents. We spoke in our room, but not outside of the female dormitory. One thing I learned about Jamaicans is that they loved to dance. We swayed our hips to one of Shakira's songs on my disk player.

Time progressed and my roommates complained about me being unclean. My roommates said my dirty clothes had been in my locker for weeks. My roommates decided they wanted a new roommate. I brought Sheila to a corner and spoke to her in private. I explained I had no knowledge of how to use the washing machines and didn't have any detergent to do laundry. My living allowance was low since I had been there for less than six months. I was unable to leave the center for trips to the stores. Sheila brought me to the laundry room and showed me how to use the machines. She also allowed me to use her detergent and taught me how to cook Ramen noodles. I told Sheila that in my country, my grandmother washed and cooked for the family. My grandmother had a washing machine though some people washed in the river. Sheila expressed her country was similar to mine.

Later Chelsey yelled, "Mi nuh wan har inna mi room!" She meant she didn't want me in her room. The resident advisor moved me to a different room.

My new roommates were Marcia, Terrica and Sabrina in the second room. Miss Vee, the resident advisor, reassured me they were kind girls. I wanted to avoid changing rooms again, therefore I spent most of my time at the gym.

In March 2001, my health declined due to lack of sleep and a poor diet. I refused to eat brunch. I had asthma and used a Proventil inhaler at bedtime.

My health improved and living allowance increased during the summer. Students signed up for trips to places such as J.C

Penny, Kmart, Walmart, the cinema, skating and bowling. I made sure my name was on the list to go off center before the list was full. I enjoyed going to the movie theatre and bowling. I watched Joe Dirt and Shallow Hall in theatres in 2001. I also engaged in arts and crafts and wrote poetry which the staff loved. The teasing didn't bother me as much and there were fewer complaints. I became friends with my Haitian Coworkers, Emma and Magdalene. I also became friends with Joanna and a Puerto Rican boy, Ricardo. My table was no longer empty in the cafeteria as we ate together. Ricardo loved a Haitian girl, Marie. Ricardo taught me Spanish and I gave him French Creole lessons. My appetite increased and I even sneaked in line for a second serving of food. I had gotten used to American food. I left my food unattended once and watched in disgust as someone spit in it. After the incident, I skipped brunch and bought a sandwich at the chapel. The chapel also had entertainment and other activities. Students played pool or card games at the chapel. I played the card games Uno or Go Fish.

In August, 2001, I completed my trade training for hotel business clerk. I worked at the cafeteria where I did community service. My punishment became my salvation. I believed I received five dollars an hour. I even recall depositing money in the bank when I went with my friends off center.

September 20th, 2001, was a traumatic day for me. My roommates Marcia, Terrica, and Sabrina invited a couple into our room. The girl, Jessica, was from the Virgin Island and James, from the Bronx. Boys were forbidden in the girls room; therefore, I reported the couple to the resident advisor Miss Kohls. James got terminated from the program the same day. Jessica remained at the center awaiting an electronic plane ticket. Jessica had only one more night with her friends.

My roommates whispered near the bathroom wall, "Snitches get Stitches." I learned what that meant that night. I was extremely exhausted, half asleep, when I got hit on the head. I could barely open my eyes when I was hit on the head thirteen times with a broomstick. I tried to defend myself, but I got bit on my right arm. My roommates were entertained by the whole scene as they watched on their beds. I weighed one hundred and fifteen pounds as tall, ebony-skinned Jessica stepped on my back with her thick leg. Jessica stamped on my back numerous times with her brown FILA boots.

The nurse at the hospital asked if I would like to press charges. Nurse Debby said, "If you don't press charges I will."

The health report was written in medical terminology. I wish physicians would refrain from writing in medical terms. I had a bite mark behind my right arm. My head had an abnormal accumulation of fluid under the skin. I had ruptured blood vessels and complained of headaches and visual disturbance.

At the hospital, the policeman took my statement and pictures of my bruises. The officer remarked that Jessica was seventeen years old., I got a seven-day medical leave of absence and Jessica got terminated. The nurse treated me with antibiotics for the bite mark on my arm. I was shocked to learn that a human bite was worse than a dog bite. I remembered where dogs placed their mouths in my country. I once saw a dog pull a dirty diaper from an outside trash can. Dogs in Dominica were treated differently from dogs in America. American dogs are pampered with love like children. I understood the reason as I contemplated the number of bacteria that must be in a person's mouth.

I had no close family members except for my aunt in New York. I called her to inform her of the incident and of my leave of absence. I avoided details of the incident. I also informed my father of what happened in the dormitory. My father made it known that he would send me one hundred dollars. The hundred dollars were to be shared between my aunt and me. I wanted to keep the whole hundred dollars.

On the 22nd of September, I rode a Greyhound bus to the Port Authority. One of Jessica's friends asked how my head felt in an unconcerned tone of voice. I ignored the girl and took the A train to Eighth Avenue, then the L train to Brooklyn. I was happy to see my family after all those years. My aunt offered me pizza and I refused since I took antibiotics and other pain medications. The nurse warned to avoid consuming milk or dairy products. I gave my aunt fifty dollars and motioned upstairs. I felt as though I was paying to stay at my aunt's house. The following day I explained in detail what I endured at the Job Corps Center.

My aunt Josephine yelled, "Job Corps sent you here to die? What if you have a concussion? My insurance cannot cover it, nuh. You're not going to die in my house. Go back to the Job Corps. You're their responsibility now!"

On the 25th of September I applied makeup, put on sunglasses, and returned to the center. Staff and students were surprised to see me.

One of Jessica's friends uttered to another girl, "I thought she was dead."

The girl replied, "She came back so I could finish the job."

I was afraid for my safety and reported the conversation to the security guards. A security guard suggested I write a statement and include the names of Jessica's friends. Three security guards escorted me to school. My English teacher, Mr. Antoine, looked at me and said, "You're a strong woman." I did not feel strong. The world was cold and so was outside. I moved to the window seat and sat there wishing I could vanish to another place.

September 27th, I spoke again to Dr. Smith. We had not spoken in the five months since I was sick. I complained about my anxiety and future at the Job Corps Center. I alienated dormmates and roommates and wanted to leave.. I am happy I refrained from leaving the center.

October 21st, I finally passed my GED exam. But I felt as though I had not earned that pass. I felt the instructor passed me out of sympathy. I suffered headaches after I got assaulted which made it difficult for me to study. Despite my misfortunes, I accomplished my goal of completing my trade and GED program. I was transferred to the west side of the first floor that was meant for "high performing students" and students transitioning to college. This side of the dormitory was a co-ed side where both men and women lived in the same hall. I met a girl from my village in Dominica and she said that the students on this floor were mature. Mature? One night a group of students watched cartoons in the lounge. The cartoons they watched were no ordinary cartoons. The students watched South Park and Crank Yankers. I never understood the words to the theme song of South Park.

In November 2001, I became an intern at the Villa Roma Hotel in Callicoon, New York. The Villa Roma Hotel was breathtaking and the people were warm and friendly. I entered the hotel and was greeted by my supervisor, Miss Laura Pendengue. My supervisor looked at me and mentioned she would feed me cake to fatten me up.

I worked in the human resources department where I provided clerical support. My supervisor was disappointed in me one day. She asked me to type something in the computer; however, my typing needed improvement. Miss Pendengue said that I typed worse than her fourteen-year-old. I got fired and she suggested I obtain advance training.

I was unsuccessful at the hotel and did my internship at the center. I worked at the shop in the chapel. Norma Coll was the supervisor who guided me at the chapel. I interacted with the students regularly. One of the advantages of being at the chapel was that my name was at the top of the list to go on trips. On December 19th, I received a certificate for outstanding performance and a good reference from Norma.

By April, I was attending Sullivan County Community College in Loch Sheldrake, New York. The Job Corps Center had a driver who transported students from the center to the college. Students also received money to buy food at the college. I chose the associates degree program with paralegal studies as my major. The classes were difficult; therefore I withdrew to social work. I struggled with math, but English and literature boosted my average.

On the first day of college, I wore a blue and white striped sweater, blue faded jeans and blue and white sneakers. I presumed the shoes just arrived in style, but a Jamaican girl on Dormitory who braided my hair revealed differently. The girl showed me her baby picture of her in the 1970's wearing the exact shoes.

On the first day of school, the most amazing thing happened! I approached the cafeteria and I saw my friend Olivia. Olivia left elementary school in the seventh grade. We embraced each other with long hugs and jumped with excitement. Olivia's major was registered nurse and we shared a science lab together. My grades were unsatisfactory and I withdrew from the class. Olivia suggested I should leave the center since I completed the program. I contemplated Olivia's advice; however, Job Corps was my main support.

I was annoyed with my roommates at the center. My roommates poured salt and pepper on my bed. When I took a hot shower, they turned the faucet on and the water became cold. My complaints were ignored. Both the resident advisor and Dr. Smith perceived I was socially unskilled and emotionally disturbed. I joined my roommate's game rather than complained. I sprinkled salt and pepper on their beds. Sleep refused to come and I was stressed. Marcia had an alarm clock which beeped every second. She blamed the noise on the snooze button. One day, Terrica played a song and I got the impression she wanted me to leave. Terrica played the song, "Get Out" by Shyne Featuring 112. I entered the room just in time to hear, "Get out what you talkin' bout, put your shoes on and start walking out." I got the point, however, I remained in the room.

In the summer of 2002, Olivia visited me at the Job Corps Center. Olivia's impression of the center was that it looked like jail.

Olivia remarked, "Aisha you need to get out of here, come stay with me."

I wanted to leave the Job Corps Center to reside on campus. Students from the center were limited at college. I wanted to socialize with friends on campus, join the poetry club, and engaged in social activities. I was excluded from those options. A driver from the center came to retrieve students from the college after the classes were done.

On July 30th, 2002, I saw Dr. Smith. Dr. Smith was concerned about me wanting to leave the center and live on campus. Dr. Smith suggested I write a list of advantages and disadvantages of leaving or staying. On August 4th, I showed Dr. Smith the list I wrote and he felt I was mature and ready to make decisions.

Then one day at the center someone yelled, "Aisha your mom is on the phone!"

I assumed my stepmother called, for when she calls I am told that my mother called. I walked to retrieve the phone mounted on the wall. I was shocked to hear my biological mother on the phone. My aunt Catherine from Saint Thomas told my mother I was at the Job Corps Center. My mother mentioned she had eleven children. I was the fourth child out of those eleven kids.

My brother Kyle also called me at the center. I informed him of my location and he was surprised. I was only three hours away from him. My brother stated he would come to get me immediately then scheduled a day to pick me up at the center. I informed Emma, Magarete and her roommate Alana. I remembered I sneaked into their room to sleep at night. We watched GIA, Bound, and Boys Don't Cry. My friends were pleased I got in contact with my mother. I forgot about college and everything else when my brother said he would come rescue me from the Job Corps Center.

My friends and roommates signed my autograph book before I departed the center. I still have my autograph book today. On the first page I wrote:

*The Job Corps was not easy to complete; however, through hard work, determination and a little confidence I made it. You have to remember what you came to the Job Corps for. Most people forget what they came to the Job Corps for and they falter.*

My friends wrote their phone numbers in my book and wished me good luck.

One cold December afternoon, my brother and his girlfriend Hazel arrived in a red Mercedes car and we drove to Rhode Island.

The Delaware Valley Job Corps Center affected me mentally and emotionally. I went to the center as a child and left as a mature, strong woman. My family was proud of my accomplishments. I received much more than what I went for. I completed my trade, obtained my diploma, gained college experience, learned Spanish, and met some beautiful people from different parts of the world. I saw Spanish people and snow for the first time. Spanish people are so beautiful, God must have spent extra time on them. I also got the opportunity to speak to my mother I have not known from eighteen months old. I spoke to siblings on the phone I never knew existed. The center did not break me. I would recommend the Job Corps to any student who wishes to turn their life around. No one experience is the same. Everything happens for a reason.

The girl who teased and read my poem aloud in class apologized to me and now we are friends on Facebook.

In the year 2020, I contacted family and friends. I was sad to learn that Vivienne Carla Maffia, who I knew as Miss Vee, died of a heart attack last year. She did not live to see her 77th birthday. Miss Vee was a sensitive and compassionate person. She made scarves and brought homemade soup for the students at the center. Ms. Vee will be missed. I was sheltered and I got a taste of the real world at Delaware Valley Job Corporation. I also got a chance to meet my extended family.

# CHAPTER 9

# *My Extended Family*

*1* lived with my father for three months then he sent me to a Job Corps Center. I referred to the Job Corps Center as a whole new world. The people, climate, food, language, and customs were different from what I knew. I saw Spanish people, Jamaicans, and Haitians for the first time at the Job Corps Center. I reunited with my friend from elementary school and spoke to my mother and siblings for the first time. Then in December 2002, I met my mother's side of the family I called my extended family.

In December of 2002, my brother Kyle and his girlfriend Hazel came to retrieve me.. The trip to Rhode Island was a four-hour drive.. We arrived in the afternoon and went to my older sister Adrienne's house. A light-skinned Adrienne opened the door with a wide dimpled smile and introduced me to the rest of the family. A seven-foot-tall Christmas tree lit the perfectly decorated apartment. I looked around and walked to the kitchen. I noticed a 2002 calendar hanging on the wall in the kitchen. The twenty-eighth day was circled on the calendar with a written note underneath. The note read: *I'm going to see my sister for the first time.* A smile in a circle was drawn at the end of the note. A smile crept my face. I watched as my siblings, nieces, and nephews danced to the music which played in the living room.

My brothers Ethan and Grant mimicked my voice and said they loved my accent. They asked me to say something to them in my language and I asked, *"Comment ça va* ("How are you?" in French)?" Adrienne gave me a Build-a-Bear Bee teddy bear which had a birth certificate. My mother gave me a fourteen-karat gold necklace with a cross. I gave my sister Adrienne a vase I molded at the Job Corps Center.

Kyle made known he had no space to accommodate me at his home. The family agreed I would live with my sister Adrienne. Adrienne lived with her boyfriend Antonio and their children Antonio Junior, Marcel, my sisters, Emerly and Hailey.

My mother visited my sister the following day and the family gathered at the kitchen table. My mind was filled with questions to ask. I asked my mother if she ever looked for me and how I came to live in Dominica.

My mother replied, "I worked at Wendy's restaurant and one day I returned home from work and you were gone."

My mother added, Adrienne, who was six years old at the time, told her that my father took me and drove away in a blue car.

Emerly and Adrienne joined us at the kitchen table and confirmed what my mother said. Adrienne mentioned it rained on that day.

My mother has eleven children, five boys and six girls and twenty-five grandchildren. My brothers are Andrew, the oldest, Kyle Junior, Ethan, Alex and Grant. The six girls are Adrienne, Emerly, Hailey, Jennifer, Audrica and me. My mother revealed that four of the children's fathers were unknown.. I called my mother a slut. I asked my mother how she could have kids and not know who their fathers were. I made my sister Emerly cry. I admit I was disrespectful. Emerly stated, we might have the same father and I angrily denied it. I called my father to confirm.

I disclosed my location with my father and he was stunned to learn my mother had other children. My father mentioned he knew my older siblings, Adrienne, Andrew and Kyle. I asked my father if he was Emerly's father. My father responded no and he then spoke of a man who could have been Emerly's father. My mother looked confused when I discussed my father's response.

My family shared stories and I spoke of my experience in Dominica and the Job Corps. My mother kicked Adrienne out of her home when she was pregnant at fifteen. My mother and Adrienne were pregnant at the same time. Adrienne was in Foster care and had the worst experience. I could sense unresolved issues between my mother and Adrienne. My mother raised eight children on her own. The three children my mother neglected to raise were Emerly, Kyle and me. Emerly was raised with her grandmother, Kyle lived with Aunt Catherine, and I was raised in Dominica.

I felt fortunate I was raised with my father's side of the family in spite of my strict upbringing. I could have been in a group home or Foster care like some of my siblings.

I was unable to bond with my sisters at Adrienne's house and I became distant. I spent most of my time writing in my journal. I wrote a poem called "Twenty years mother." I entered the poem in a poetry contest and won out of three hundred people.

I felt comfortable talking to Kyle, probably since I saw him in Saint Thomas. Kyle took me out of the house when Adrienne and Antonio fought. Adrienne stayed home with the children while Antonio worked at a furniture store. Antonio cooked when he returned home and I washed the dishes.

One day while I was cleaning the dishes, Adrienne yelled, "I do not want a dishwasher, I want a sister I could talk to. You were not what I expected to show up at my door!"

Adrienne and I fought in her kitchen one day. I aimed a knife at my sister hoping she would surrender; however, she came towards me. My sister assaulted me and I called her a "psycho bitch."

My mother who stood there warned, "If you're gonna pick up a knife, you better be prepared to use it!"

In February 2003, a man named Javier visited us frequently. Emerly explained Javier was a friend of the family. Adrienne confessed, though she was with Antonio, she loved Javier. Adrienne made known she and Javier dated as teenagers and attended the same school.

Javier was the only friend I had in Rhode Island. Javier grew feelings for me which made my sister jealous. I explained to Javier we should only be friends. Javier stated he had a one-night stand with my sister, but she slept with his best friend. Adrienne got pregnant by Javier's best friend and told Javier the baby was his which broke trust between them.

On Valentine's Day, Javier brought me a bouquet of real roses with a mini teddy bear inside. Javier said that he wanted me to know that he was real. Emerly took the bouquet of flowers and placed them in a vase of water on the table. Adrienne saw the vase of flowers and her face lit up.

Adrienne with a bright smile sounded like an excited little girl, "Is that for me?"

Emerly answered, "No Javier brought it for Aisha."

Adrienne's expression changed from excited to angry and she shook the floor as she stomped off to her room. She looked like a disappointed little girl who neglected to receive a Christmas gift from Santa.

I cared little for the flowers. I should have mentioned the flowers were for Adrienne; however, that would have caused conflict between Antonio and Javier.

I rode in Javier's white, Chevrolet Malibu car one day and Adrienne tailgated Javier. Adrienne drove a red, petit cruiser and tried to drive Javier off the road. Javier stated he would drive into an area where Adrienne's van was unable to fit. Adrienne tailgated Javier; however, he drove past her.

One day I tried to cross the road in a four-way intersection and a red petit cruiser speeded towards me. The driver in the red petit cruiser almost ran me off the road. I wrote the license plate information on a paper then headed to my mother's house on River Street. I spoke to my mother about what happened and Ethan and Hailey confirmed Adrienne was the driver. I mentioned to my mother I would inform the police.

Ethan interrupted, "What are the police going to do? In our family we don't involve the cops; we handle shit ourselves."

I could not believe the response I got for my sister's attempt to kill me. The Job Corps Center accepted teens from sixteen to twenty-four years. I was twenty years old and after the incident, I wanted to return to the Job Corps. I never imagined I would be far from home with family who were strangers to me. I now believed my father tried to protect me from my family.

The living arrangements with my sister was a catastrophe and my mother's house was the next option. Adrienne took back the Build-a-Bear she gave me and demanded I pay her electric bill before I left her house. I received a few thousand dollars for the completion of the Job Corps program. I left Adrienne's house and I lived with my mother and younger siblings, Ethan, Grant, Jennifer and Alex.

In the spring, I visited my aunt in New York. I rode the Greyhound bus for nine hours since the Greyhound bus was not an express. According to my aunt, I made excuses and rejected a job offer. My aunt had plans on helping me find a job and continue my education. Sometimes when we are young we make unwise decisions that we later regret. When I returned to Rhode Island, Javier picked me up from Providence and drove me to my mother's house.

I became depressed and isolated myself from everyone.

One day my mother exclaimed, "You come here expecting something like I owe you something. You act like you're better than everybody, like your shit don't stink!"

My mother continued saying, "It's not my fault your daddy came and took you away!"

To be honest, my mother was right. I acted as though she

owed me twenty years of her life. I acted as though she owed me twenty Easters, birthdays and Christmases. I received no card or phone call. My mother kept replenishing the earth, bearing more children in this world after I was separated from her. I learned to appreciate the way I was raised within the three months I lived with my mother.

My brother Alex came home with a pair of sneakers he stole from the mall one day. Alex showed the sneakers to my mother, explained how he got the sneakers, and my mother laughed. My mother's response bothered me. My aunt would have punished me. My aunt would have brought me to the mall to return the sneakers and apologize for stealing.

The children had no curfew in my mother's house. I remembered my mother refrained from eating for a whole day as she waited for Alex. My mother sat at the kitchen table in the dark with a worried look on her face. My brother Alex, around twelve years old, returned home at four in the morning. My brother got disciplined; however, my mother admitted it hurt her more than him. My mother felt bad for raising her hands on Alex. I compared my mother to my aunt in Dominica. I did not do half of the things my siblings did, yet I got beat for anything. My mother received a letter in the mail which notified her that Grant was absent from school for thirteen days. Where was Grant when my mother assumed he was at school? My mother never asked the question. My mother stated the statement was a typical error and my brother's ADHD (Attention Deficit Hyperactive Disorder) was the reason for his absence. I decided to acquaint myself with the stranger who was my mother rather than to pass judgements.

I caught my mother in a daydream and I sat with her at the kitchen table. My mother said she tried to contact me when my father worked at Fredenhoi on boats in Saint Thomas. My mother stated she made numerous attempts to speak with my father at work, but he hung up the phone. My father told his manager to hang up the phone if my mother called. This meant my mother knew where I was all these years. The first day we spoke my mother mentioned Adrienne informed her that my father took me away. I asked my mother again how I ended up in Dominica.

My mother answered, "Your father came to visit. Your father said he was going to bring you to visit family in Dominica, but never brought you back."

"Why didn't you call the police? I asked.

"That's your dad. I did not want to call the cops on your dad." Mother replied.

Twenty years is a long time for a mother and a child to be unable to bond and form an attachment. I asked my mother who named me, for no questions were too silly to ask. My mother uttered, when she was pregnant with me her African friend told her to name me Aisha. My mother thought of naming me Jezelle.

My mother and I spoke of our upbringing. My mother spoke of how she feared her mother and ran away from home.

My mother uttered, "My mother threatened me with a pen knife and I ran away then she sent boys to look for me. When the boys found me they brought me to my mother and she beat me with an almond tree branch that cut up my skin."

My mother explained to me why she avoided corporal punishment to discipline the kids. My mother was afraid of hurting her children.

Mother explained, "They do things to make me mad. I want to hurt them so I don't hit them."

My mother discussed how her mother wanted to know the reason why she kept running away. My maternal grandmother assumed something was wrong with my mother and brought a man who looked Russian to perform witchcraft on my mother.

"The man placed me in a tub naked, I had to look to the ocean. I was twelve to thirteen years old." Mother added.

That revelation sent chills down my spine and made me wonder. Was I cursed?

For the brief time I lived with my mother I became depressed. I missed my menstrual period for three months. The doctor explained stress, a new environment, and climate was the reason for my absent menstruation. My crazed sister Adrienne's frequent visits were unwelcoming.

One day as I walked to my mother's house, Adrienne drove by me. When I arrived at my mother's house an angry Adrienne waited for me to enter. I slowly entered the house and Adrienne grabbed me by the hair and knocked my head on the walls of the house. My sister's explanation was that I saw her and I did not wave at her.

My mother shouted, "Not in my house, take it outside!"

What happened that day motivated me to find a place of my own. I presumed my mother's house would be safe, I was wrong. My mother's house was an unsafe environment for me due to my sister's violent behavior.

In the spring of 2003, I placed my belongings in boxes. I left my mother's house and moved to a shelter on Sayles Street in Woonsocket, Rhode Island.

CHAPTER 10

# The Shelter

I left my mother's house in the spring of 2003 and moved to a shelter in Woonsocket. I approached a white building with blue doors and a dark man greeted me at the door. I mentioned I wanted to keep my stay at the shelter confidential. The man stated for safety reasons, staff refrained from disclosing information to anyone about a person being at the shelter. Shelter stays were limited to ninety days. The staff at the shelter extended someone's stay based on progress. Curfew was at nine p.m. on weekdays and twelve p.m. on the weekends. Javier and I went to the movies at the Lincoln Mall on the weekends.

Residents did chores and signed a permission slip to leave the center for overnight visits. At the shelter, program fees were assessed based on income. Employed residents gave thirty percent of their income to reside at the shelter. The unemployed residents performed community service. I did community service and saved the money I earned from the Job Corps Center to secure housing. Permanent housing was difficult to obtain since housing properties had a long waiting list. I lived at the shelter; therefore, my name was at the top of the list for emergency housing.

The shelter helped with basic needs, support, and job search. The staff allowed residents to use the telephone in the office to check the status of jobs or apartments. The office had an area where residents obtained food, clothing, or books locals donated. I took the most appealing clothing or books to read. A staff member knocked on our room doors and woke us every morning to look for work and housing.

Woonsocket is such a small city that you never know who you are going to run into. One day I left the shelter and went for a walk. Adrienne drove slowly behind me and I quickened my steps. Adrienne rolled her window down and voiced that she was not going to hurt me. I hesitated, then proceeded to get into Adrienne's vehicle. Adrienne said that Javier had returned to his ex-girlfriend Sasha and I was a rebound. Adrienne insisted on taking me to Sasha's house. Just like Adrienne told me, Javier's car was packed on the side of Sasha's house. Adrienne dropped me off and I motioned to the house. Javier looked at me with such disgust that I wanted to leave. But Sasha's mother was friendly and invited me into the house.

Sasha's family, Javier, and I sat at the kitchen table sipping a drink of water. Sasha wanted to know when Javier and I started dating. I made known that Javier and I started dating in February. Javier stood up from his seat, leaned over, and tongue kissed Sasha in front of me. I sat there and imagined a truck driving at maximum speed to run me over. Sasha brought me to her room and showed me things that Javier bought for her. She also showed me poems Javier wrote to her in Spanish. I was surprised he wrote poetry. I left Sasha's house and walked to the shelter. The shelter was a short walk from Sasha's house. Who could blame Javier? Sasha was a beautiful, dark woman with a stable, accepting family. My family was dysfunctional; a fact that led me to the shelter in the first place.

At the shelter, eating, sleeping and bathing became difficult.

I found out what I was experiencing was called depression. In America there is a pill for everything. A doctor at the Thundermist Health Center prescribed me Zoloft. I consumed Zoloft for about a month and strange things began to happen. My eyes deceived me. Zoloft numbed my feelings, but I was unable to trust my own sight. I saw and heard things that were not there. One of the residents explained I was hallucinating, one of the side effects of the prescribed drug. I spoke of the side effects to my doctor and she ended the medication. The doctor prescribed me Paxil CR, but I refused to consume other medications. I was afraid of the side effects. I focused on seeking employment, finding my own place, and leaving the shelter.

I lived with five women on the third floor of the shelter. I lived with Judi, Ruth, Nora, Rochel, and Carmen. Judi was a thin, white, elderly woman and Ruth was a chubby, white girl. Ruth was the youngest of the group. Nora was a pregnant Spanish girl who braided my hair at the shelter. Rochel was an African woman. Carmen spoke of her daughter often. Carmen taught me how to dance bachata and how to cook at the shelter. The first time I cooked rice, the rice looked like pudding. One weekend Carmen and I went to a Portuguese restaurant. I could not stop talking about how delicious the food was. When Carmen and I stayed at the shelter, we taught Ruth how to walk properly. Ruth shook the whole floor when she walked.

One day I twisted Ruth's long blonde hair and we searched for work. Ruth said that her aunt worked at the city hall and she would help us find work. Ruth and I walked to the city hall and a truck drove by with guys who shouted, "Jenny Craig!" Ruth raised her middle finger and cursed the guys with the big F word. I was embarrassed and walked faster in front of her. I pretended I was not walking with Ruth.

"One eight hundred Jenny Craig bitch!" echoed in the air as the truck drove away.

Ruth introduced me to her aunt at the city hall. Ruth's aunt was pleased she made a friend and gave me a job referral.

In the summer of 2003, I worked as a camp personnel at Cold Spring Park. I notified Tasha Roberts; my transitional specialist assigned to me from the Job Corps Center. I distributed snacks, played games, and provided activities for children at the camp. I wore a light, blue t-shirt with the name of the park written on it along with long, black pants for my uniform. I loved my summer job and working with children. One funny moment was when a squirrel stole my slice of pizza and ran up the tree to eat it. Unfortunately, my job ended when the summer ended.

Staff extended my stay at the shelter for a short time. I had to leave the shelter after I stayed there for seven months.

I contemplated on finding shelter somewhere else; however, I was informed the shelter in Woonsocket was better. Other shelters were unsanitary with bad living conditions. I called my uncle to discharge me from the shelter. I stayed with my uncle throughout the winter of 2003.

I have only positive things to say about the shelter in Woonsocket. The staff were friendly and treated me with respect. The staff connected me with a program called Family Resources when I left the shelter. Family Resources helped me with the security deposit and first month's rent. April 1st, 2004, I had my independence, my first place.

I lived in a studio apartment at Plaza Village Apartments in Woonsocket. The basement apartment had a long walk-in closet and a large window in the living room and kitchen. My apartment was in a muted area, peaceful, except for the birds chanting. My neighbors were two, white elderly women who lived across from me. The cost of living was low. I lived in subsidized housing where I paid thirty percent of my income. The United States Department of Housing and Urban Development paid the rest of the subsidy.

In April 2004, I obtained employment at a retail store called A.J.Wright. The best part of the job was interacting with customers regularly. Everything in my apartment was from A.J.Wright. My living room was decorated with bold colors of burgundy and gold. I made a wine decoration in my kitchen. What I loved was a bicycle shaped wine rack I bought at A.J.Wright.

One day another manager offered me a job. The manager commented on how she loved my interaction with customers. She wanted me to be a waitress at her coffee shop for five dollars an hour. I got paid seven dollars an hour at A.J. Wright. The manager explained the pay was low since Wednesday nights were cruise nights. Employees received two hundred dollars in tips on cruise nights. I was tempted but remained loyal to my job at A.J. Wright since I worked with a great team.

Friday, May 21st,I had an interview at a Mexican restaurant called Taco Bell. I worked at Taco Bell in the morning from eight to two for seven fifty an hour. I worked at A.J. Wright from five in the afternoon to when the store closed at eleven or midnight.

I had my own place and two jobs. I was no longer depressed and Javier had moved on. I had no one to turn to except for the family who I avoided. I decided to try to heal old wounds.

# CHAPTER 11

# Healing Old Wounds

*D*oes time heal old wounds? My mother moved from River Street to Sweet Avenue in Woonsocket. I loved the convenient location despite the traffic noise. I also welcomed the pleasant aroma of fresh bread across the street.

My younger siblings greeted me when I arrived at my mother's house. My mother seemed surprised to see me. My mother had a singing motion wall mounted fish which hung on the wall. Big Mouth Billy Bass entertained as it sang, "Take me to the river, drop me in the water." My brother Grant loved dancing to the song.

My mother was happy she had a man in her life. My mother's boyfriend Kevin reeked of cigarettes and smoked like a chimney. Kevin was a tall, dark man with a dark past. He served years in jail for sexual assault and his son was really his grandson. My mother was aware of his past, yet she remained in a relationship with him. My mother said that he was the only man who did not abuse her or disrespect her. The children had little respect for Kevin but tolerated him. One day Kevin mentioned Alex stole three hundred dollars from him and left the house.

I visited my mother often and became acquainted with my family. My mother looked sophisticated. An outfit was never complete without complementing jewelry. My family's skills and abilities defined who they were: artists, singers, chefs, dancers, and a designer. My brothers could dance and Hailey drew extremely well. My sister Audrica had skills in braiding hair with or without extensions. In my family, those who could neither sing nor dance had gifted hands. Adrienne was the most talented person in the family. Adrienne could organize weddings, baby showers, make holiday reefs, arrange bouquets, and decorate a house to perfection. Adrienne could also dance. My mother was an artist and a chef. My mother sat at the kitchen table one day and made a birdhouse out of popsicle sticks. My mother cooked like a chef and she and my aunt planned on managing their own restaurant one day.

One day my mother, the kids, and I watched the movie "Soul Food" at my mother's house. My mother decided she would bring the family together by having a soul food dinner every Sunday. On Sundays, everyone placed their differences aside and gathered at my mother's house. We gathered at the kitchen table to eat collard greens with smoked neckbones, cornbread, mashed potatoes, chicken, and bacon with cabbage. This palatable meal could ease any tension in a room or calm a savage beast. After dinner we placed a second plate of food aside to take home. Sometimes we went home after dinner or we sat in the living room to watch a Tyler Perry movie. My family is a huge fan of Tyler Perry. We saw the trailer for "Madea Goes to Jail" on television. The majority of the family gathered money together to watch the movie at the cinema. We had a great time at the cinema and the tension subsided. Most of the tension came from Adrienne and me. I tried to heal old wounds yet there remained a scar as a reminder of how I got wounded in the first place. Adrienne was that scar. My sister reminded everyone of how she assaulted me a year ago.

I have heard it said that blood is thicker than water. Family does not have to be blood. People who care and support you can be family as well. The church can be family.

My mother attended The Church of God and Prophecy in Providence. A driver from church transported her to Sunday service. Sometimes we attended The First Baptist Church.

# CHAPTER 12

# Spiritual Life

> "Just as a candle cannot burn without fire,
> men cannot live without a spiritual life."
> — *Buddha*

My family attended the First Baptist Church on Sunday mornings. This holy sanctuary was where troubled souls met to worship. Men were equal, sharing a religious bond.

The sisters in Christ conducted a soup kitchen in the basement of the church. The sisters fed and clothed the homeless, the needy, and the greedy. My mother and my Aunt Grace cooked at the church for Sunday fellowship. My mother came with the kids and Adrienne came with her husband and kids. My aunt who has eight children brought her youngest children Celess and Ronald Junior. Larry drove the church van to transport people to church. I rode the church van to church on Sundays.

I believe in a higher power. I love listening to testimonies and voices uniting, singing to God. I am filled with joy when a person could reveal what God has done for them. I thanked God for waking me up in the morning. Having food on my table and a place to sleep was a blessing. The song I learned in Bible school was, "He got the whole world in his hands." Adrienne led the children's Sunday school choir. I have no knowledge of how to organize a children's program. I loved being in the church choir. I was not as gifted as a white, blind lady who sang in church. This lady was blind but was blessed with a voice superb like Celine Dion. Maybe I am exaggerating, but she did have a beautiful voice.

Larry Led the youth choir at the First Baptist Church. My aunt Grace organized the choir with members of our family when Larry left the church. We called ourselves The Redeemers. My aunt said that was when she redeemed herself. Our choir had no gowns, but we coordinated with gold tops and black skirts. One odd lady joined us to sing; however, we considered her as family. My aunt's daughter Celess led most of the songs with her high, soprano voice. Later, everyone in the choir had a chance to shine. Audrica, Celess, and I sang soprano while my mother and aunt sang alto. Emerly and my other cousins blended into the background. My aunt included her son Ronald in the choir so he would not feel excluded. Though Ronald could not sing, my aunt believed he would be the next Ruben Studdard. Ruben Studdard was the winner of American Idol in 2003.

Choir rehearsals were held on Fridays. Choir members rehearsed at my aunt's house or at the church. We brought the church alive when we sang songs by Kirk Franklin and other lively artists. One Sunday we sang "I will Follow Him", the Sister Act version. I sang the soprano part and the second verse to the song "Mercy Said No." We sang hymns of praise, like hallelujah before the pastor gave his sermon. Members of the church ate together and enjoyed fellowship at the end of service.

Time progressed and the church had a handful of members in the congregation. The church decreased in members and our choir ended. We felt discouraged and were not fully commit-ted. I was informed the church had maintenance issues. The First Baptist Church was no longer lively; therefore, my sister Audrica and I visited a Spanish church called Monte Calvario (The Calvary Worship Center).

The Calvary Worship Center started with approximately ten people then increased in members. The church was lively with members singing in English and Spanish. One of the songs we sang was "Amigo de Dios (Friend of God)".

The church arranged a car wash to raise money for a bigger building one weekend. Drivers gave generously any amount of money they could afford. I yelled "Lava tu caro" on the side of the road as people brought in their vehicles. A man brought in his extremely filthy vehicle. One could have sworn he splattered mud all over the vehicle on purpose. The church raised a lot of money that weekend.

A deacon transported me to church on Sundays. Sometimes my mother wanted me to accompany her to church in Providence. My mother continued to attend the church her mother took her when she was a child. The rest of the family accompanied my mother to church on special occasions like Easter and Mother's Day. My mother was proud to introduce me as her long, lost daughter at church. Church members knew my siblings since they were babies. My maternal grandmother was a God-fearing woman, though she was strict. My grandmother taught the kids to pray before bed and read their Bible often. I missed the opportunity to meet my grandmother, she died October 21st, 2000.

I failed to have a home church and went back and forth between churches. I loved the energy and vigor of the Calvary Worship Center. I embarked on my spiritual journey. I found comfort in knowing that to be spiritual does not require attending a place to worship every week. However, having a place to worship strengthens your faith. I believe God allows things to happen to us so we could turn to him. God has a way of testing us and we could turn that test into testimonies and trials into triumphs. When God closes a door, keep that door closed.

CHAPTER 13

# An Uninvited Guest

*J*avier was at the door and he looked like an unshaved home-less man. I invited him inside and we spoke for a while. Javier told me that Sasha left him for a man in the army. Javier also said that he shared an apartment with a girl in Providence to be close to his job at Bank of America. Javier was forced to leave his apartment after he got fired at his job.

I felt embarrassed as I walked with Javier on my way to work. Javier's sneakers were ripped open. I bought Javier a pair of shoes and he took advantage and asked for shirts and socks. Javier explained that his brother took his belongings. I bought Javier what he wanted despite my complaints.

Javier came to my apartment to watch movies like he did before. I told Javier about his brother and me before he heard the story from someone else. I had met Javier's brother at the Calvary Worship Center. He drove me home from church and a simple ride home turned into a one-night stand. One innocent kiss turned into a night of sex.

Javier sounded disappointed, "Aisha why did you break the

code, why did you sleep with him? My brother has always been jealous of me, he wants everything I have."

Javier paced around with his hand on his head. "It's not your fault you were taken advantage of."

I was not taken advantage of and I refused to believe Javier's brother was jealous of him. I should have left his brother alone; however, I was unable to undo what was done.

Javier complained about his parents. Javier's parents allowed him to drive the car when he worked. His parents took the car from him when he was unemployed. Javier complained he had no privacy and slept in the basement with the dogs. I suggested we should live together, but he refused.

"I can't leave my parents' house, it's too expensive to live on my own. My mom doesn't speak English very well. I have to be home to read the mail and answer the telephone." Javier explained. Javier made it known that no one in the family could help.

Javier visited often, especially when he had an argument with his parents. I felt insecure with Javier since we had an unstable relationship. Javier and I decided we would be friends. I was not lonely, I had two jobs to occupy my time. I worked as a cashier during the day at A.J. Wright. Javier also was employed at A.J. Wright one time. At my second job I worked from three to eleven p.m. as a certified nursing assistant.

# CHAPTER 14

# *Certified Nursing Assistant*

*I*n August of 2005, I worked at a rehabilitation center as a certified nursing assistant. The job paid ten dollars and seventy-five cents an hour for an eight-hour shift with a one-dollar differential. Families entrusted their loved ones to us in this large nursing home. I was delighted to be part of the committed staff. My presence was valuable for both staff and residents depended on me. I worked stable hours and worked the same days every week from three to eleven p.m. I worked on the first floor during the week and worked on the north or south side on the weekends. I helped patients with daily activities such as feeding, bathing, and toileting. I answered patients call signals, transported patients to and off beds, recorded vital signs, and distributed snacks. I did evening care from seven to nine p.m. before I left work. Patient progress was documented, signed, and reported to the charge nurse.

I walked about half an hour to work every day and an African man named Mamadou drove me home at night. Mamadou worked hard to support his family in Africa. He worked over fifty hours a week and said his patients were his family.

One of my weaknesses was that I regularly got attached to the residents as I cared for them. In this profession, it is unwise to become close to the residents. When the residents pass away, you feel as though a family member died.

I grew attached to a fragile lady on my floor named Doris. I saw myself in Doris. I believed I would become like Doris when I grew to an elderly woman. This ninety-year-old lady signaled the call light often which annoyed most staff. I answered her call signal since most of the time Doris just wanted to talk to someone. Doris showed me her photo album and spoke of her house and modeling career in the 1940's. I looked at her photos and saw that Doris was gorgeous and slim. Her beauty did not fade as an elderly woman. Doris reminded me of my grandmother who was sophisticated and felt younger than her age. The problem with Doris was that she was convinced she could do simple tasks like waking from bed to use the bathroom. Doris knew she was at risk for falls; however, she was stubborn. Doris refused to ring the call signal when she needed help.

One day I asked, "Doris, why didn't you ring the call light?"

Doris replied, "I didn't want to bother anyone, you CNAs work so hard."

I mentioned to Doris that her safety was important and it is okay to bother us. I felt concerned and spoke to my coworker. I told her to supervise Doris when I was absent.

I was off from work one day and returned the following day. My coworker informed me that Doris was admitted to the emergency room. Doris fell and broke her hip. When Doris returned from the hospital, she was no longer an assist. Doris needed complete care. She was transferred to another floor and her health declined gradually causing her death. In less than a week I had a new patient on my floor in the room where Doris used to be. I was sad about the situation and avoided getting close to the residents after that.

I had more compassion towards the combative residents. I realized the combative residents were the ones whose families neglected them. The nurse transferred me to another floor and I had a resident named Mr. Parker on my assignment. One of the employees warned that I should be careful in caring for this patient since he bites and punches. I approached Mr. Parker and spoke of my involvement in church. Mr. Parker had a discontented look on his face. He said that his son is a pastor who is too busy to visit him. What a small world; I knew the pastor. The man I cared for was the father of the pastor of my church.

I expressed my concerns to the pastor when I attended church the following Sunday. The pastor smiled and I saw a young version of his father standing before me. The pastor visited his father at the nursing home and the resident attitude changed. Mr. Parker was less angry. I felt happy to see the pastor and his father laughed and talked. Mr. Parker and I became like old friends. Sometimes the little things you do can make a big difference.

I took care of a few combative residents. One day an obese lady mentioned she would slap me back to Africa. This lady only smiled after a weekend home visit with her husband. An employee suggested I sing the song "Daisy" since she loves it. I approached the lady to do her care. I sang, "Daisy, Daisy, give me your answer, I'm half crazy all for the love of you." The resident calmed down as she finished, "But you'll look sweet upon the seat of a bicycle built for two." I felt as though I was caring for children in adult bodies.

Another day I accompanied an employee to care for a resident who moved her bowels. The resident was combative, so I needed another aid to help me. The resident took her hand, pulled out a ball of feces, and placed it in the aid's pants pocket. The white aid looked blue at that moment and I wanted to vomit. A nursing assistant job is not for everyone. As compassionate or caring as you may be, you will need a strong stomach.

I graduated from the nursing assistant program on September 23rd, 2005 and became a certified nursing assistant on October 27th, 2005.

In the fall of 2005, my life changed. I vomited at work and a coworker asked if I was pregnant. I presumed I ate expired food from the vending machine. A stomach bug was epidemic in the nursing home, too. I became nauseous as I passed supper trays to the residents. The supervisor ordered me to leave work and to return when I felt better. The supervisor explained that I could not care for sick residents if I was sick myself. I went to Thundermist Health Clinic for a checkup. The nurse took my vital signs and asked about my last menstruation. I informed the nurse of my irregular period. I urinated in a cup for a pregnancy test and told her that I need medication to return to work.

When the nurse returned she explained, "I am not able to give you medication for what you have. Congratulations you're pregnant."

The charge nurse gave me permission to leave work; however, the registered nurse fired me over the phone. The registered nurse said that I neglected to call or show up to work. I explained I had permission to leave then she gave me a number to call when I was ready to work. I needed a letter from my doctor stating I am physically able to work; however, I had some complications and my doctor refused to grant me permission.

My deepest regret was returning to work after I gave birth. I could never forget that particular day when I tarnished my license.

April 2007, I floated from my floor to a floor where I was unfamiliar with the residents. The staff gave me an assignment with no reports on the residents. I looked at the names and room numbers on my assignment. I knocked on each resident door to introduce myself. I needed to know what time the residents wanted to get ready for bed.

An aid named Gail asked, "Do you have Peggy on your assignment?"

I did not know Peggy. Gail informed me that Peggy was Miss Joseph and it was seven p.m.

Gail explained Ms. Joseph has a urinary tract infection (UTI) and that her family has her on a strict changing schedule. I told Gail that I was in the middle of taking care of someone else and they should have informed me from the beginning.

"Leave what you're doing and I'll come with you to change Ms. Joseph. She uses a Hoyer lift. Now that I have time I am coming to help you." Gail added.

I left my unfinished task and accompanied Gail to Ms. Joseph's room.

"I do not want to be in bed when my daughter comes," uttered Ms. Joseph.

Ms. Joseph refused to be placed on the bed to be changed so Gail and I proceeded to report to the registered nurse, Kathy Johnson. We wanted to know how to handle the situation.

The registered nurse stated, " Ms. Joseph cannot be changed in bed at seven, then put back to sit in the chair for when her family comes to be placed back in bed at eight. We have short staff and it is very busy. What Ms. Joseph is asking for is impossible. When you change her brief, she will have to remain in bed."

I reported to Ms. Joseph what I was instructed to do and she disagreed. I explained I was doing what I was instructed to do by the nurse. I worked under the license of a registered nurse. I explained to Ms. Joseph that I would do what the nurse wants me to do. One thing I learned is to never argue with a resident. Another employee, Miss Mathews entered the room and suggested I should step out of the room to avoid an argument. Miss Mathews left the room to get assistance from a male employee. Miss Mathews and the male aid lifted Miss Joseph from the chair and placed a clean brief on her. Miss Mathews looked at me and uttered she was all set.

Miss Joseph's daughter arrived and Ms. Joseph told her daughter that I refused to change her brief. Ms. Joseph's daughter was not pleased and reported me to the charge nurse. I explained I followed instructions from a superior nurse, Miss Johnson. When Miss Johnson was confronted, she denied the conversation and I got terminated.

April 4thwas my last day of work at the rehabilitation center. I obtained a reprimand on my license for neglecting to change a resident's brief.

I believed Miss Johnson wanted to keep her job. It was her word against mine. The registered nurse Miss Johnson worked at the nursing home for about eighteen years. I was a young employee who had much to learn. The problem is that the reprimand on my license will never go away. My license will be tarnished forever. I could only work as a certified nursing assistant if someone disregards the reprimand or if I have a letter of good report from previous employers. I learned that the residents are always right. One thing for sure:

> "They may forget our name, but they
> will never forget how you made them feel."
> — *Maya Angelou*

CHAPTER 15

# Pregnant at 24

On August 1st, 1995, my menstrual period had been absent for two months. My aunt was concerned and brought me to be examined by a doctor in Roseau, Dominica. The disappointed look of people's eyes fixated on me at the maternity ward. I was at the maternity ward in my school uniform. An Indian doctor scanned my stomach in the examination room. The doctor stated I had an ovarian cyst on my right ovary on the lining of my uterus. Surgery was unnecessary. The doctor performed an Xray and viewed my pelvic organs. The doctor came to the conclusion that I would be barren. My aunt and I left the hospital after the procedure. My aunt sympathized with me and said, one day I will find a husband who would be willing to adopt children.

Ten years later, October 2005, I discovered I was eleven weeks pregnant. Sometimes in life, what you ask God for comes at an inconvenient time. I wanted to have a steady income and further my education. I contemplated on how I would break the news to my family. I called my father in St. Thomas to inform him that I was pregnant.

My father sounded disappointed, "You just went and messed up your life. I hope you're not going to become like your mother."

My stepmother overheard the conversation and added, "Don't let this accident happen to you again."

They spoke to me as though I was a pregnant teenager.

I joined my family for dinner one Sunday afternoon. I confessed I was pregnant when my sister Audrica claimed she dreamt of fishes. Most cultures believe that seeing fish in dreams is a sign of pregnancy. My mother asked about the child's father since my relationship with Javier ended. I admitted though Javier and I were not in a relationship, we were intimate.

On December 16th, 2005, Javier accompanied me to my prenatal testing at the hospital. I was stunned by the sonograms the doctor showed us of the baby. I mentioned that the portrait of the baby resembled an alien which angered Javier. My prenatal tests were normal except for abdominal pains and heartburns. I figured my mother would know what to do.

I seeked advice from my mother who gave natural birth to eleven children. My mother went through what I experienced eleven times. I believed my mother was strong beyond her years. I was fascinated by my mother and Adrienne's pregnancy stories. When my mother was pregnant with Jennifer, Adrienne was pregnant with her daughter at the age of fifteen. I laughed when she showed me how she danced pregnant. I tried to conceal the baby's gender; however, my mother guessed I was having a boy. My family neglected to plan a surprise baby shower since no one can keep a secret in this family.

The whole family was the guest at my baby shower. Adrienne and her family were present including other siblings, nieces, and nephews. My sister Audrica discovered she was pregnant at my baby shower. I received baby shoes and pacifiers from Hailey. Andrew gave me Bible story books and a teddy bear. My mother cooked and organized the baby shower and Adrienne arranged the basket. A coworker at A.J Wright gave me a bassinet, car seat, bathtub and highchair. I had everything I needed including the expensive stroller from Javier's mother. The only thing Javier gave me was grief.

Some tasks are difficult to perform when a woman is pregnant. Such tasks include picking objects off the floor or leaning forward. Javier was at home one day and an item fell on the floor in the kitchen. I asked Javier to pick it up for me since I was unable to bend forward.

Javier replied, "No, I'm not walking on eggshells just because you're pregnant."

Cleaning the house, bathing, working, and walking to do grocery shopping became difficult for me.

I had a tall basket of dirty clothes to wash. Javier said he would bring the clothes to his mother's house since they had a washer and dryer. Javier placed the basket of clothes in the trunk of his car. The dirty clothes remained in his car for a week. I called to remind Javier that I needed clean clothes for work. Javier arrived at my apartment the following day and dropped the basket of dirty clothes onto the rug in my living room.

"I have nothing clean to wear for work tomorrow." I explained as he walked away.

"That's not my problem!" Javier exclaimed as he slammed the door behind him.

The following day I went to work at A.J. Wright with dirty clothes on. I was unable to report to an employer I have nothing clean to wear for work. I complained to my mother about Javier.

My mother said, "You sure know how to pick them."

I received my paycheck, and Javier and the dirty laundry were still present. I walked down the hill to the laundromat and was stupid to ask Javier for help again. I carried the heavy basket of clothes and was forced to hold the laundry detergent with a few fingers. Javier took the laundry detergent from my hand and watched as I struggled to carry the heavy basket down the hill. Two years had passed since I slept with Javier's brother. Javier knew I was carrying his child. Javier was no help and I allowed him into my home to use and abuse me.

One snowy afternoon, Javier was at my apartment. I received a termination notice for my electricity. I needed to call the electric company to set a payment arrangement plan. I asked Javier if I could use his cellular phone to call the electric company.

Javier responded, "Here's fifty cents go use the pay phone outside." Javier wanted me to walk in the snowstorm outside to use the pay phone.

I shouted, "Since you're so selfish get the fuck out of my house before I call the cops!"

"By the time the cops get here I'll be long gone!" Javier replied.

I became stressed with headaches, heartburn, and abdominal pains. I got terminated at the nursing home and I struggled financially. I applied for unemployment and waited for temporary Disability income (TDI). This income arrived late and I received an eviction notice. I appeared in court and avoided eviction. The judge ordered me to pay a sum of money. I was unable to move into a two-bedroom apartment until the rent was paid in full.

I received TDI later and was able to pay my bills. I missed the weekly paychecks and wanted to attend college. I spoke to my aunt Grace on the phone about my plans to have an abortion. My aunt stated that I would regret that decision and suggested I forget about Javier. My aunt made known I had family support. I was scared as one day Javier revealed he dreamed I died giving birth and he had to raise his child alone. Did he dream that or was that what he hoped for?

My mother accompanied me to one of my prenatal checkups. The doctor instructed me to keep off my feet for a while. The doctor advised me to be a couch buddy, eat every three hours, and avoid overwhelming myself. The doctor noticed that I strained myself. The doctor asked if anyone at home could help me. My mother told him that we have a huge family.

Audrica, Hailey, and Ethan were the ones who helped me at home. Ethan stayed with me for a while to help until he found a place to stay. Depression and pain took a toll on me and I refused to go through pain for nine months.

I went to Thundermist Health Center and spoke to my doctor about obtaining an abortion. My doctor explained I was twenty-two weeks pregnant, too far along to have an abortion. I expressed my concerns about my depression and having little support. My doctor discussed placing me in physical therapy. She explained I was weak and needed to be physically strong to give birth. The doctor explained that visiting nursing assistants would assist me after the baby was born. I was informed that the baby weighed two pounds and I needed to gain weight.

I returned home after the doctor's visit to watch a soap opera called "As the World Turns." An actress called Lizzy was pregnant in the soap opera. I felt emotional watching the soap opera and cried when she cried. watched a movie called "Riding in cars with boys" starring Drew Barrymore when the soap opera finished. I got the idea to throw myself down the stairs. I threw myself down two flights of stairs. A short, white lady upstairs heard the noise and came to my aid. The lady called 911 and I was admitted to the emergency room. I informed the doctor that I fell down the stairs. The doctors were more concerned about the baby. The doctor placed the stethoscope on my stomach to listen for a heartbeat. The doctor said that everything was fine.

Two weeks later, six months pregnant, I endured strong contractions and was rushed to the hospital. I felt relieved my mother was with me. The doctor was convinced I was ready to give birth.

I repeated, "No I'm not ready; the baby is only two pounds."

"You might not be ready, but the baby is ready," said the doctor as he went to get the equipment.

I removed my johnny and got dressed. I was reluctant to give birth so soon and left the hospital with my mother.

One spring afternoon, I walked to Shaw's Supermarket to buy groceries. I felt an intense pain through my leg and back and collapsed near a tree. My uncle's girlfriend drove by and stopped when she saw me on the ground. She asked if I was okay and saw that I was pregnant. I asked if she could drive me to the supermarket. The woman took me to the hospital instead.

My water broke when I arrived at the hospital. I was four centimeters dilated. I had six hours of contractions and an hour and half of labor. I pushed out a five-pound, eight-ounce baby. The doctor called the baby "Guapo," Spanish for handsome. "Baby Boy Felix" was what the doctor wrote on the incubator since I neglected to have a name for two days. I loved the name Zion, but that was my nephew's name. Javier named the baby after his grandfather Enrique. Adrienne and Hazel were the first people who visited my apartment to see Enrique Valentin.

Javier and I went to court the following week. Javier wanted documentation for his mother to verify the child was family. Javier demanded a paternity test, though he knew he was the child's father. Javier explained that his mother was heartbroken when she found out another child she grew attached to was not family. The child was not his brother's child, yet his brother paid child support for the child. Javier was pleased with the paternity test results.

In less than a week, Javier arrived at my apartment and demanded I wear appropriate attire. I was shocked when he fixed my hair and chose an outfit for me to wear. Javier adjusted his own clothing in the mirror. I asked Javier why he mistreated me when I was pregnant.

Javier's response was "Tough love."

If what I experienced was tough love, I wondered what hatred felt like.

Audrica was at my apartment that day making goofy faces in the mirror. Audrica overheard Javier was taking me to his mother's house and asked to accompany us. Javier refused her company. Audrica assumed he denied her company since he knew she understood Spanish. My sister Audrica was right. The visit to Javier's parents' house was just a means to convince me to give my son to his parents.

Javier and his parents spoke Spanish in the kitchen. I wish Audrica, my Salvadoran sister, was present to translate. Javier and his mother stared at me as I changed my son's diaper.

Javier uttered, "You see ma, she doesn't even know how to put on a Pamper."

Javier's mother brought me into the living room and spoke in her Spanish accent.

Javier's mother, Teressa, tried to persuade me to give her my son and I could work and attend school. I presumed she held my best interest and wanted to help me. I contemplated the idea until Javier spoke.

Javier interrupted, "Not like that, you have to give my mother full custody, give up your parental rights!"

In not so good English, Teressa added, "You his mother; you can see him anytime."

Javier shouted, "Keep the boy, stay on welfare, and struggle with him or do what you have to do and everybody will be happy!"

"I'll struggle with my son," I said with an attitude. That day was the beginning of my years of struggle.

I should have known better than to ask Javier for anything. One day I asked Javier for money to buy Pampers and he told me to use duct tape and paper towels. The white elderly woman who lived upstairs gave me ten dollars. The woman's husband had passed away and she had no children of her own. Angels come in different shapes and forms. Javier wanted me to know what it was like to struggle. I tried to dismiss the fact that I tried to take my son's life in the womb. God was in control for my son and my life. I monitored his development as I kept track in a baby's memory book. Can you believe it? The boy's first word was sex at nine months. I was sure he meant to say six for I was counting, but Jennifer and I heard the same word. At eleven months the word "dada" expelled from my son's mouth before "mama," to my dismay.

One day, Jennifer came to visit and at thirteen months old, Enrique struggled to communicate.

Jennifer said, "Aisha he's speaking Spanglish."

Enrique yelled, "Shut up!"

Both my sister and I burst with laughter.

My son was my world as the years progressed. I became my son's Easter bunny, tooth fairy, Santa Claus, and his light in this dark world. I tried to end his life, but he was my life, my reason to live.

The following year, 2007, my baby and I moved out of our studio apartment. I rented a two-bedroom apartment at building forty-one in the plaza. My son and I had our own room; however, I missed the tranquility of my old home. What I did not miss were the memories I left behind.

Maya Angelou, American poet and civil rights activist once said, "When someone shows you who they are, believe them the first time." Javier showed me who he was from the beginning, I just did not open my eyes to see. The only thing we both could agree on was that Enrique was the best thing that happened to us. The doctor predicted wrong and God had the final answer. I dealt with the challenges of being a single mother and the obstacles life through in my path.

CHAPTER 16

# Obstacles

Sometimes single mothers make sacrifices and take risks. Life fails to give us what we want and we are faced with obstacles.

I was unemployed; however, I had the most important job in the world. This full-time job as a mother came without instructions. I tried to be the best mother I could be. My biggest stressor was being unable to find a suitable day care center to place my son. Javier's aunt baby sat my son when he was about five months old. She was certified and the Department of Human Services compensated her through a program. I got fired from my job and Javier's aunt no longer cared for my son.

Two years later, I found a day care center near me called Connecting for Children and Families. This program accepted children from prenatal to age five. I searched for work while my son was at the day care center. The director from the center called me one day and said that I need to return to retrieve my son. The woman explained that my son had difficulty expressing himself verbally and as a result he hit the other kids in frustration. The woman suggested my son should return when he could communicate better.

I stayed home with my premature son who had speech difficulties. At my son's age he was supposed to be speaking at least a few sentences. I placed my son in a program called Early Intervention. The Early Intervention program was a service that assisted babies and toddlers with developmental delays or disabilities. Every Wednesday one of the workers visited my home to help my son with his speech. The woman said his speech problem could be the result of him being born premature or because he hears two languages being spoken. My son's father spoke Spanish at his home and my English needed improvement.

As time progressed, my son was able to speak a few sentences. One day I placed my son in his SpongeBob stroller and walked to the Shaw's Market.

My son saw a pineapple and pointed, "Look mom, Stobbob house!"

At McDonalds, my son asked the cashier for a krabby patty. I bought my son a happy meal. My son's favorite television show was SpongeBob. I decorated his room with the Bikini Bottom bedroom set and stuffed animals.

My only source of income was a monthly welfare check of four hundred dollars. I received a Rhode Island Food stamps card with three hundred dollars' worth of stamps. I saw why people thrived on this lifestyle; however, I refused to live like this.

From 2008 to early 2009, my son re-entered the Connecting for Children and Families day care program. My son loved day care so much he refused to leave. The staff was great with the kids. The welfare department paid for the day care service but warned I should obtain employment to keep my son in day care. I obtained a monthly bus pass through my medical insurance. I used the bus pass to ride the public bus and look for a job.

A thrift store called Savers opened for business at A.J. Wright's location. A crowd of people stood in line as they waited to be recruited. I was one of the fortunate ones to receive employment. I worked as a production worker from eight in the morning until four in the afternoon. I unboxed and tagged items to be displayed in the store. Most of the items were clothing to be tagged and priced. The men unloaded the trucks. My salary was seven dollars an hour. A weekly paycheck was better than receiving four hundred dollars on the first of every month. I remembered I made that amount in a week as a certified nursing assistant. My reprimand was recent so I was unable to find employment in the healthcare field. What I liked about being a production worker was that I had the perfect mother's hours. Production workers worked during the week and had the weekends off. I requested to have Wednesdays off due to my son's early intervention service. My manager granted my request; however, I returned on Saturdays to perform the unfinished task. My manager explained she wanted to be fair with everyone. My manager, a tall, white woman was relieved to find empty racks when she returned to work on Monday.

I took a risk when I allowed my mother to watch my son on Saturdays so I could work. My mother's boyfriend Kevin, a sex offender, had a "red flag" with the Department of Children Youth and Families (DCYF). Kevin was on fifteen years' probation and had to be supervised around children. Some of my siblings visited my mother often so my son was not left alone.

My son improved his speech and development and further early intervention was unnecessary. I discussed with my manager about changing my schedule and working regular hours. My manager disagreed and admitted she was pleased with my schedule. She added everything worked out.

My son had strep throat at day care one day. The doctor gave me a written excuse allowing him to stay home for three days. I asked my mother if she could babysit so I could work.

My mother replied, "Sick children belong with their mothers. Mama got to have a life too."

My mother was unconcerned about the fact that I risked termination if I called out of work. I called out of work and informed my manager; I would submit the written excuse from my doctor. My manager accepted the doctor's excuse and placed it in my file, then gave me a written warning. Obstacles were always in my path.

I woke up with a swollen mouth one day due to my wisdom tooth. I called my manager at work to discuss this issue and explained I was unable to work.

My manager responded, "You have a tooth to take care of, but I have a business to run. Sorry, you're fired."

Just like that I was fired over the phone. A co-worker who lived in the building across from me insisted I should pursue legal action. He thought the manager was unprofessional to terminate my employment over the phone.

I filed for unemployment and was scheduled for a hearing. I canceled the hearing due to another hearing I had on the same day with DCYF. I presumed the hearing with the Department of Children Youth and Families was more important. I feared losing custody of my son.

I watched my son one afternoon as he rode his toy car outside. A police officer approached me on the step and asked questions of my negligence. The officer told me that he was informed I left my son unsupervised on the street. I became furious and the officer commanded me to calm down. The officer took my statement and left. Someone said that my friend Carla called the police. I looked up and I noticed Carla and her friend standing in front of the window upstairs. I became angry when I saw a cordless phone in Carla's hand. I threw a rock at the window where Carla and her friend stood.

I yelled, "Come outside!"

Carla cried, "No I'm scared."

Adrienne stood next to me and said, "Leave her alone, something is wrong with that girl."

Though Carla was mentally disabled, she was still capable of making a phone call. What bothered me was that child protective services was now involved.

A woman from the DCYF office called me. The worker said that it would help my case at the hearing if I could obtain letters from everyone in the building. The letters were to state that I am a good mother. The woman added that if someone could testify and say that they have never seen my son unsupervised, it would help my case. No one wanted to get involved so I typed a letter and asked willing tenants to sign it.

My mother accompanied me to the DCYF office in Providence. We rode two buses and walked a long bridge to reach our destination. My son remained in my custody; however, the report remained on my record for three years.

I returned home after the hearing and vented to Hazel about what had happened. Hazel said that I should insert feces in an envelope and place the envelope at the front of Carla's door. We both laughed and I pondered the idea. I looked for bird or dog feces outside to place in an envelope. Then I contemplated another plan. I buzzed Carla and her friend's door for two weeks at one in the morning to harass them.

Carla, who hid in her apartment, came outside one day. Hailey, one of my sisters, called me to report that Carla was alone and had gone to the laundromat. I took a knife from my kitchen, hid it in my pants, and placed my shirt over my pants. I entered the laundromat where Carla was and pulled out the knife. I chased Carla with the knife like a crazed woman.

I jumped on the counter and yelled, "If they took my son from me you would end up missing!"

Carla said her friend upstairs called DCYF. I calmed down, hid the knife, and ran home.

Carla's husband abused her. One day he broke her arm and threw her outside in the cold at two in the morning. I was the one she buzzed to let her inside. I invited Carla into my home and placed myself in danger. My heart beat as hard as a drum when her husband knocked on my door and asked for her. I lied to protect her and said Carla was not there.

In the morning, Carla called the police about her husband and he was arrested. The same night Carla came to my apartment and cried that she missed her baby. The following weekend,

Carla, my son and I went to the Stadium Theatre to see Shrek III. Carla was like a big kid and I wanted to put a smile on a friend's face, not knowing that friend would betray me.

Carla's friend moved out of her apartment. Carla bailed her husband out of jail and he continued to abuse her. I kept my distance but called the police to report a disturbance. I stopped calling the police when I realized some women would rather be abused than be alone. I went from feeling anger towards Carla to feeling nothing but sympathy for her. Who was I to judge? My son's father treated me like crap yet I kept returning to him.

I stopped worrying about Carla and focused on obtaining employment and furthering my education. In life, obstacles hinder you from fulfilling your goals. All you can do is get bitter or get better.

# CHAPTER 17

# Get Bitter or Get Better

*"Pray until something happens (PUSH)."*
*— Karani Ken Ranii*

In 2009, my New Year's resolution was that I hoped things got better by getting easier. Who said life was easy? Life is not a bunch of roses and even roses have thorns. Sometimes you just have to push and pray until something good happens for you.

The Department of Human Services sponsored a nursing program for food stamp recipients. I tried to enroll in the program; however, I was unsuccessful. Marsha Schmucks, the program coordinator at the Community College Of Rhode Island, loved my resume. She suggested I obtain a referral from my case worker to be eligible for enrollment. I asked my caseworker for the referral and she denied the request. My caseworker explained that I already had a nursing license that I wasted. I figured if I could not attend college through the department, I would pay for the courses on my own. Marsha Schmucks said that classes cost nine hundred dollars. Nine hundred dollars was beyond my budget. I received a monthly welfare check of four hundred dollars. I searched for a job and prayed for things to work out for me that year.

My caseworker at the welfare office said that in order for me to continue receiving assistance, I would have to enroll in a job search program or engage in something productive.

I enrolled in the Rhode Island Works job search program at the Department of Labor and Training Center. I called this job center network, "job search boot camp." A job search log was to be delivered weekly to a vocational worker. The vocational worker requested confirmations such as emails or business cards from employers who received my applications. The Rhode Island Public Transportation Authority bus was my only transportation besides my legs. What took other clients five to ten minutes to get to with a vehicle, took me hours on a bus. I was unable to travel to many places in a day to apply for work. The vocational worker mentioned she did not receive adequate job search from me and I was terminated from the program. I was as relieved as I felt discouraged. How would the workers know what it is like to find a job? Many of the workers have been working in the same position at the same location for over five years.

Opportunity knocked and I answered. I saw a commercial about Lincoln Technical Institute which offered different programs. I had the opportunity to receive new training and skills. I wrote the telephone number of Lincoln Technical Institute on a piece of paper and called for information. The receptionist informed me of when classes started.

On February 17th, 2009, I enrolled at Lincoln Technical Institute in Lincoln. I chose the medical assistant program. I woke up at five thirty every morning to get prepared. I brought my son to my mother's house at six thirty, then rode the bus to school. My mother's house was not the best option, but the Department of Human Services denied my request for childcare assistance as I was unemployed. I compensated my mother because she made it possible for me to obtain my education. I remembered my father saying that I ruined my life when I became pregnant. Having a baby made things difficult, but not impossible.

The winter was harsh as I traveled with my son early in the morning. The first thing I bought when I received my income tax refund was a car. Gregory, an ex-coworker of mine from Savers, sold me his 1996 Ford contour for eight hundred dollars. Gregory said he would accept six hundred dollars if he could use the car when needed. Gregory also mentioned he would teach me how to drive. I believed his deal was reasonable. Gregory's daughter Samantha attended Lincoln Tech as well and drove us to school.

At Lincoln Technical Institute I studied medical terminology, anatomy and physiology, electronic medical records, phlebotomy and other subjects. I loved the courses and I learned to read doctors' prescriptions and practiced writing prescriptions. For example, the abbreviation for two times a day is B.I.D. One of my challenges was phlebotomy since I feared needles. How could I insert a needle in someone's vein when I feared being injected? The instructor made me practice on mannequins before I drew blood from anyone. I discovered I had rolling veins and some students had what they called "junkie veins"' the best veins to draw blood from. I passed the written phlebotomy exam; however, the instructor felt I was unprepared. I repeated the class and passed with a B average. I controlled my nerves during the phlebotomy practical exam.

Thanks to Samantha I had good attendance and was punctual in class. I was just ashamed I was unable to drive my own car. What I should have done was obtain my driver's license before I bought the car. I had a learner's permit. I read the driver's manual on the way to the Department of Motor Vehicles and passed the test.

One day after Samantha drove me home from school, she borrowed the car. Samantha got into a car accident and was lucky she avoided being hit on the driver's side. An officer explained that Samantha was at fault for the accident since she drove the maximum speed on a four-way lane. This was the consequence for the decision made of just handing over my car keys. I felt as though the car was not mine. I was just thankful Samantha was not hurt. I went to Gregory's house to look at the damaged car in the driveway.

Gregory asked, "Do you want the car fixed or your money back?"

I thought about the winter months and I knew I needed the car. I regretted my decision to fix it. Gregory said he knew a mechanic who could fix the car for a reasonable price.

The car received a fresh coat of burgundy paint and the windows were fixed. I took the car to the mechanic for an inspection. The mechanic stated the car had fifteen hundred dollars' worth of internal damage. I saw a car with duct-taped windows on the road, yet my burgundy car with Betty Boop seat decor failed inspection.

Kevin, my mother's boyfriend, suggested I should take the car from Gregory. Kevin offered to drive me to school and teach me how to drive. I asked Gregory for the car and he asked for two hundred dollars. I had no intentions of giving Gregory two hundred dollars, but Gregory threatened to hurt me if I refused to give him money. I gave Gregory the balance I owed based on our agreement. I should have allowed Gregory to keep his car and give me my six hundred dollars. The car looked appealing on the outside but was messed up on the inside like some people I knew. What made matters worse was that the car had a mind of its own. When Kevin stepped on the brake pedal the car moved and the oil pressure gauge indicated an oil change was needed when no change was necessary. The gas meter read the tank was empty when the tank was full. Despite these setbacks, I made it to and from school. I wanted to drive my own car, but Kevin drove me places instead of teaching me how to drive. I decided to take driver's education.

I contacted Lee's Driving School and spent my fifty dollars learning to drive for an hour. The instructor grew impatient and frustrated with me. I crashed into a pole as I tried to park the car. The instructor suggested I should find someone to teach me how to drive instead of wasting money on driving school.

I spoke to Kevin about my experience at driving school and he chuckled, "I'll have you driving in no time." I was nervous to drive on the road. I was so nervous I held the steering wheel with both hands.

Kevin had a driver's license therefore he drove me wherever I needed to go. We went fishing at Stump Pond Lake sometimes. Kevin drove me places often and became too comfortable. Kevin flirted and harassed me for sex constantly in the car. I presumed he was joking and laughed, then he said, " I'm serious as a heart attack."

Kevin said, "Let's go parking, just one time, nobody has to know."

I felt uneasy and disregarded his sleaziness. When I ignored him, he placed his hand on my thigh. Kevin had gangrene on one of his fingers and a doctor amputated the finger at the local hospital. What began as a splinter could have been treated. When he placed his hand on my thigh I noticed he had a small knife in the car he used to peel his mango with. I took the knife and I placed the sharp edge of the knife on Kevin's remaining fingers.

I said to Kevin, "If you touch me again, I will cut off the rest of your fingers and send them to my mom as a birthday present." That was the first and last time he touched me with his repulsiveness, but he still verbally harassed me. I never learned to drive.

I gave up spending money on the car to keep it running efficiently. I was unable to pay my mother to babysit. I did the inevitable.

In June 2009, Javier and I had a court hearing. Javier offered to live with me to watch our son while I attend school. Javier mentioned I would not have to pay him to watch his son which could save me money. Javier gave my son his first haircut and took him fishing with his uncle. My son caught his first fish. Javier mentioned I placed school before his son. My son was the reason I attended school. I wanted to advance in my education to qualify for better jobs to be able to support our son and avoid being dependent on welfare.

October 19th, I started my clinical externship at Thundermist

Health Center. I longed for employment there; however, God had other plans for me. On December 30th, I was placed at a new site called Adult Primary Care and Pulmonary Medicine. I prepared the examination table for the podiatrist, Dr. Hart. I scheduled, confirmed appointments, and performed clerical work. I interacted with patients regularly. Unfortunately I needed more experience to obtain a job there.

In February 2010, I completed my internship and received a good reference letter. On February 3rd, I graduated from Lincoln Technical Institute with a 3.55 average. I should have gotten a 4.0 because I worked extremely hard.

Javier was disappointed in me since I failed the most important exam, the Registered Medical Assistant Exam (RMA). I could have had a medical assistant license instead of a medical assistance certificate of completion. Javier said I wasted my time, but I refused to believe that. I accomplished a lot and received knowledge that could be applied anywhere. I could do phlebotomy, CPR, EKG, write prescriptions, perform vital signs, and more. I do not regret education; however, I placed myself in debt. Currently I have two loans to pay. The money was disbursed twice and the loans are not consolidated. As for my car, the car lasted sufficient time to take me through school. The sad news was that the tow truck took my car and I received one hundred and twenty dollars for my car.

I asked for a hearing at the welfare office to plead for childcare assistance again. I explained that the school I attended was vocational and could lead to employment. I added that I was acquiring new job-related skills. My case worker at the welfare office approved childcare assistance. I failed to receive employment, but I prayed until something happened. I pushed hard enough and I got an opportunity to work at a senior center at the Alternative Adult Day Care Center.

CHAPTER 18

# The Adult Day Care

*I*n April 2010, I applied at Saint Rita's hospital, but the hospital was not hiring. I spoke to Miss Carol Johnson, the volunteer coordinator, about volunteering. Miss Johnson informed me that I could only volunteer at the center for three to four hours a week. I needed to volunteer for more than four hours a week. My caseworker at the welfare office said that I needed to volunteer for twenty hours a week in order for my son to remain in daycare. Later, my son was not the only one who attended daycare.

On Friday, April 23rd, I volunteered at the Woonsocket Senior Center in the Alternative Adult Day Care. I rode the bus to work. I volunteered four days a week from nine to two in the afternoon. Every morning I hung the clients jackets, prepared the tables for breakfast and lunch. and planned for the day. I gained knowledge of this country when the staff played trivia games with the clients. I was amazed at how intelligent the elderly were. My favorite memories were the activities I participated in with the clients. We played card games, danced, exercised, and played bingo. Once during bingo, a man yelled, "sixty-nine!" An eighty-year-old man wiggled in his seat and said, "Ooh that's my favorite number!" Work was never boring. I also painted and colored with the clients. I found these exercises rather relaxing, probably too relaxing. Clients painted pictures for me and I made clients sign their artwork, then I took their artwork home.

A lady named Gloria was the genius who led art therapy. Human beings use ten percent of their brain; however, I believed Gloria used more than ten percent. I saw why Gloria was hired. Gloria constantly had ideas of things to make with the clients such as bird houses, floral bouquets, table mats, paintings and more. What was amazing was that she used her own money to purchase the supplies. The smiles on the clients' faces were rewarding enough when they took their art home. I enjoyed working with Gloria.

Every day of the week had a different pleasant surprise. On Tuesdays, a lady came to offer beauty service. She painted the ladies nails and styled their hair. On Wednesdays a man came to play guitar and sang songs. Thursdays became the best day of the week. I danced the twist, hand jived, and performed Zumba. Staff and clients danced to music of the sixties and seventies. I did not feel like I was working. On Cinco de Mayo, I dressed like a cowgirl and clients had their Mexican hats. What a pity, I missed Christmas with the staff. I was informed the staff dressed like Snow White and the Seven Dwarfs.

Another activity they performed was regular exercise. When clients and staff were not bouncing a huge ball back and forth we danced. The nurse made staff and clients perform the chicken dance and cha cha slide. On that day, when I returned home, I danced the chicken dance for my son. I clapped and shook my butt and my son burst out with laughter. After I danced, we watched "Jimmy Neutron: Boy Genius" then we both did the chicken dance. Both my son and I enjoyed day care.

At the adult daycare, I felt I was working when I supervised a lady with schizophrenia. I kept her occupied when I colored with her, although she wrote numbers all over the paper. This lady kept me on my feet since I could not keep my eye off her for a second. I looked away from her once and she stole someone's coffee from their table. If I was not careful, she would have eaten someone's food. I ambulated the lady and listened to her stories. The job was not difficult. I believed if I maintained good attendance, I would become a regular staff. One aid mentioned to me that she got paid for what I did for free. I was not bothered by what the nurse said. I was doing something productive with my time which kept my son in day care. Most people will work anywhere because their job pays the bills. I wondered what it would be like to get paid for something I enjoyed. I enjoyed working at the senior center. I applied for employment at the senior center; however, the director of nurses referred me to another agency since she was not hiring.

The director of nurses gave me a number of a homecare facility to contact. The woman she referred me to loved my resume, but I failed to get hired due to lack of transportation.

I prayed until something happened and something did happen for me. My caseworker at the welfare office informed me that I may be eligible to receive payments. I received bi-weekly payments of eight dollars an hour through an agency called Southshore Rehabilitation Center. The welfare department called my work experience substitute employment. Unfortunately, the substitute employment program only lasted six months.

October 23rd was my last day at the senior center in the alternative adult day care program. God does answer prayers. At the day care center, I made a friend.

In the next chapter I am going to talk about a woman I befriended at the senior center. I believe we do not meet people by accident. God sends people in your path for a reason. I am going to talk about my friend Naomi.

# CHAPTER 19

# My Friend Naomi

"We don't meet people by accident.
They're meant to cross our path for a reason."
— *Kathryn Perez, PHD, Associate professor*

I met a man named Alfred Thompson at the alternative adult day care. I sat with Mr. Thompson until his daughter arrived to retrieve him. Mr. Thompson's daughter Naomi was obese, yet she looked flawless in her black dress.

Naomi invited my son and I into her home. Naomi's home was warm and inviting and her father's big smile brightened the place. Naomi lived in a three-bedroom apartment with her father who had Alzheimer's and her three-year-old son. I knew Naomi was going through a difficult time. We both needed support.

I helped Naomi do chores in the house. I did such a good job helping her clean the house that she asked me to pretend to be her maid to impress her date one evening. I agreed to be Naomi's maid. I did the laundry and cleaned the house.

"You missed a spot, Tysha!" Kyle yelled as I cleaned his room.

Kyle returned from foster care after he had an accident. According to Naomi, Kyle was diagnosed with separation anxiety. I believed Kyle just missed his mother. Naomi was unable to lift a leg as Kyle followed her like a dog on a leash. I helped Naomi prepare for inspection. I cleaned packs of sugar, stale food, and ants. I felt like a black maid working for a rich, white woman.

Mr. Thompson was pleased when he saw how immaculate the apartment was in the morning. He spent most of the day in his room as his interest lied in soap operas. I always presumed that only women watched soap operas. Mr. Thompson improved in mobility during the time I spent helping the family. Mr. Thompson walked with his walker rather than moving around in his wheelchair. I saw the happiness in his eyes when his daughter was happy. I spent most of my time with Naomi and her family and felt like part of their family. I believe family does not have to be blood related.

Mr. Thompson spoke of his young life and Naomi's mother. The family from Trinidad inherited a tremendous amount of money when Naomi's mother died.

Naomi and I went to a clothing store which carried no plus sizes. I longed for a rock to hide under when Naomi walked into the store. The staff looked at Naomi like she was lost. Naomi looked in my direction and explained she was shopping for me. She also said that she had money to spend. I felt like Julia Roberts in the movie "Pretty Woman." One of the women approached me from behind the counter and showed me outfits to buy. I was amazed at how the staff attitudes changed when they heard the phrase "money to spend." Naomi spent about three hundred dollars in the store that day. Naomi bought me a faux leather jacket and skirt, boots, and undergarments. I realized I needed the money more than those items. I returned some merchandise including the undergarments. Naomi spent money as though money grew on trees.

I spent Thanksgiving of 2010 with Naomi and her family. We bought food rather than cook. Naomi and I never made the Trinidadian rum cake we planned to make. One of the things I loved eating during the holidays is rum cake. I loved rum cake after Naomi introduced me to Jamaican food.

Our favorite place to eat was at a Jamaican restaurant on Atwells Avenue. Naomi spent one hundred dollars on Jamaican food one afternoon. We bought Jamaican rum cake, curry goat roti, callaloo, sorrel, and other dishes that would make your mouth water. The owner of the restaurant told me that Naomi spent eighty dollars at the restaurant in the morning. One hundred and eighty dollars is a lot to spend on food in one day. Naomi disliked the comment I made about how she spent her money. I explained how the money could have paid my electric bill. Naomi responded that I was upset since I had no money to spend. I avoided telling Naomi how to spend her money except when someone took advantage.

Naomi introduced me to a few interesting people. I went on a date with a white man named David. I was not attracted to David; however, we had good conversations. David spoke of his job building computers and mentioned his cat once saved his life. David was supposed to be on the flight the day the World Trade Center got destroyed. David said his cat chewed the cord of his alarm clock and he missed his flight. He called it luck. Maybe it was not his time to die.

Naomi had a huge smile when I arrived at her home one afternoon. Naomi was excited about a man she wanted me to date. She introduced me to James, a man who was sitting on the edge of her sofa. Naomi felt I worked too hard and I needed to meet people and have fun. I agreed to go to the movie theater with James. I wore a faux leather jacket, leather skirt, and high heel boots. James and I went to the Lincoln Mall Cinema. James, about four feet tall, jumped out of the van.

"If I knew you were so short I wouldn't have worn my high heel boots."

I was unaware those words poured out of my mouth. I presumed those words were only in my head. James looked embarrassed and I walked past him in a hurry. We stood in line and chose the movie, "The Town" starring Ben Affleck.

James complained to Naomi about the comment I made about his height.

Naomi sounded disappointed. "I don't believe you. What if the man said he didn't know you were so black?"

I managed to laugh. I had no excuses.

I decided to take a break from dating. Men were interested in Naomi despite her four-hundred-pound size. I babysat Kyle while she went on dates. I remembered a day she mentioned going on a cruise ship.

Naomi's home was like my second home. I neglected my apartment which needed my attention and my son said that he felt he had to share me.

Naomi and I argued one day. I forgot what we argued about, though I suggested she should find someone else to work for her. I wanted to call her after a week but my pride got in the way.

A few months later I returned to Naomi's home feeling shameless. Naomi's home looked clean and organized. Naomi made it known that she tried to do a little for herself.

Naomi sounded excited, "Girl I lost two pounds!"

"What did you do, you took your shoes off?" I asked.

I regretted the response I gave Naomi when she spoke of her weight loss. Every loss is an accomplishment for an overweight person.

Naomi's money was finished and her friends were gone. She bailed a man out of prison hoping the man would be with her; however, the man returned to his child's mother instead. She explained how she spent money on the man and his aunt. I asked if she was an ATM machine. Naomi is self-confident and has a big heart: a big heart that could be taken advantage of.

Naomi helped me in my time of need, yet when she came to me for help, I shut her out. You cannot help someone when you need help. I was depressed. Naomi and I remained friends until the end of 2011. Mr. Thompson was admitted to a nursing home in Trinidad and always asked about me.

Naomi was my friend, boss, and my family. I was in a difficult situation and struggling financially when she met me. I was a volunteer at the alternative adult day care when I met her father. Seeing her father rise from the wheelchair and take steps made me realize why I love working with the elderly. People we come in contact with can have an impact on our life. We can change their life or they can change our life. Naomi crossed my path for a reason.

Naomi and I both suffered from depression and we tried to help each other. She wanted me to accompany her to Trinidad. I thought about the idea; however, what difference would it make? Would I have been happier? No matter where I go I will still be me. I would just be me in another place. I would have to get up and do something for myself; like Naomi's father who got up from the wheelchair and took a step. The truth is, if you fail to make a move, rise from where you are, you will remain in the same place. Sometimes it takes another person to help you get to where you want to be. Sometimes all it takes is one step.

CHAPTER 20

# A Step Up

*I*n the spring of 2011, I decided to take a step up and pursue a career in the medical field. I joined the Stepping Up Health Care Exploration Program at the Family Resources Community Action Center. This twelve-week certificate program provided training for people with low incomes seeking employment in the healthcare field. This program included seven weeks of class-room training preceded by five weeks of internship at healthcare locations.

My sister Audrica called me one day on my lunch break.

Audrica voiced, "Ma's heart stopped, we're all at the hospital and you're the only one missing."

I called Kevin to elaborate and confirmed what I heard. Kevin said that my mother had a stroke and was transported to Roger Williams Medical Center. Kevin and I rode three buses to Roger Williams Medical Center to visit my mother the following day.

I was speechless to see my bloated mother on life support. I was unaware I cared about her until I saw her lifeless body on the bed. Kevin made it known that I could talk to my mother even though she was unconscious. He warned I should say positive things to her since she could hear me. I uttered words of encouragement and of opportunities the program offered.

A panting Kevin mentioned at the bus stop that my mother's children killed her. Kevin blamed my oldest brother Andrew and sister Adrienne for my mother's condition. Kevin explained that my mother asked my siblings to transport her to the hospital and they refused. According to Kevin, my siblings gave my mother different pain medications. They gave my mother Percocet, Tylenol and Vicodin rather than transporting her to the hospital.

Naomi drove me to Roger Williams Medical Center to see my mother the second time. When we arrived at the hospital, ladies from my mother's church were just leaving. The ventilator showed that my mother was breathing thirteen percent on her own. What happened was my mother had a stroke but was diagnosed with pancreatitis and hypothermia. My mother had gone to the local hospital with a nosebleed and bled uncontrollably when she returned home. Who would have thought a simple nosebleed could lead to major complications?

As for me, I completed the Stepping Up Exploration Program. I joined a group of students to intern at Landmark Medical Center. The other group of students were sent to Thundermist Health Center. I believe we were in groups of six. I was one step in the door; however, I failed to receive a job offer. The hospital chose a man who resembled Rod Stewart to work for their company instead. Regardless, I valued and savored the experience. I increased my knowledge and was among the nine students who graduated from the program on May 23rd, 2011. I was proud of myself that I stepped up; I made progress.

I was not the only one who stepped up, for my mother stepped up as well. My mother was pronounced dead three times and escaped death three times.

The last time I visited my mother at Roger Williams Medical Center, most of the family was present. The family is big so we entered my mother's room two at a time. I bought my mother a stuffed Jamaican parrot doll in a boutique at the hospital. The stuffed parrot doll sang the Bob Marley song "Don't worry." I presumed the stuffed doll would be better than a boring sympathy card. That was the last time I saw my mother at the hospital. My mother was then admitted to a nursing home in New Bedford, Massachusetts.

The Redeemed Christian Church of God, a Nigerian Pentecostal church, was supportive. The pastor brought me to visit my mother at the nursing home after church on Sundays. Church members gathered at her bedside as they laid a hand on her and prayed.

The pastor uttered, "By his stripes we are healed."

This verse was taken from the book of Isaiah 53:5 in the New King James Version of the Bible.

One Sunday at church, the pastor announced that one day my mother would get better and walk into church. And to my astonishment, one Sunday, my mother did limp into church. My Aunt Grace and I agreed that my mother's song should be "Mercy Said No" by CeCe Winans.

My mother was unaware I visited her often at the hospital. My mother had no recollection of anything that happened. I asked her if she had nine lives.

My mother responded, "No, it is by the grace of God I am alive today."

My mother missed the opportunity to support and connect with me from the age of eighteen months. I got to know my mother as an adult at the age of twenty and had difficulty bonding with her. I alienated my mother and my siblings. I saw my mother cling for her life on life support and realized I do not want to lose her.

What I learned is that you have to be grateful for what you have before it becomes what you had.

# CHAPTER 21

# November 9th, 2011

On November 9th, 2011, I woke up to the sound of the fire alarm. I ignored the alarm and closed my eyes. I assumed someone probably burned their food.

A man yelled, "Fire, everyone, get out now!"

The sound of residents running down the stairs reminded me of the stampede in the Lion King movie. I ran to wake my son. Someone pounded loudly on the front door. My son was wrapped in a blanket with no shoes on his feet and I lifted him from bed. I grabbed my purse on the couch then ran outside to escape the smokey air. The firemen arrived and evacuated the building.

My neighbor Carla cried, "My husband is still inside sleeping!"

A fireman brought the man outside unharmed. Another fireman asked residents to form lines and provide their names and valuables they left behind. A few residents walked out of their apartments with their flat screen televisions. The firemen told everyone we would be able to retrieve valuables and belongings after they contain the fire. Residents planned to return to their apartments the following day.

I turned around and saw a group of residents talking among themselves. I invited myself into their conversation. The residents were furious. A man who lived upstairs from my basement apartment said the fire started on the third floor. The man explained that two toddlers around the age of four and five started the fire. He said the boys' parents were in their room smoking marijuana while the boys tried to light a candle in their rooms. From what I understood, the youngest boy lit the match, burned his finger, then threw the match onto the rug. You guessed right; the rug went up in flames. How could I be angry at a four and five-year-old? After all, my son was five years old.

I hid in the crowd to avoid speaking to the reporter as she questioned a few residents. Javier came and took my son from my arms.

Javier said, "I'm taking him to my house, you're homeless, Aisha."

I did not need to be reminded that I was homeless.

Residents from building forty-one and forty-five were worried about where to live or with whom to stay with. Time waited for no one as afternoon approached.

The American Red Cross allowed residents to stay at the Holiday Inn for five days. Where would residents go after five days? Would they get kicked out of the hotel to sleep on the streets? There were questions I was unable to answer.

The welfare department gave residents an electronic food stamps card to replace food loss. Residents from building forty-one and forty-five evacuated their buildings due to the power outage. I felt the most sympathy for tenants at building forty-five. Tenants in building forty-five were not affected as much as tenants in building forty-one.

Tenants were consumed with anger.

One man exclaimed, "I am going to take pictures of residents sleeping in their vehicles and call the news. The woman with the little boys better stay hidden!"

I heard the boys' parents were brought to a safe place since residents threatened to cause them harm.

A Spanish girl, Camilla, allowed me to live with her for a while. I slept at Camila's apartment and we watched a Tyler Perry movie, "Neighbors From Hell." I needed to laugh and get my mind off my homeless situation.

The following day Camila and I walked to my building and her friend arrived with a vehicle. Camila's friend was there to help transport anything I could save from my apartment.

I entered my basement apartment and dropped to my knees in anguish. My ceiling, which looked like a large piece of wet, torn, white painted cardboard was on my couch. My fish tank was used to collect water which dripped from what was left of my ceiling in the living room. I felt as though I was about to have a nervous breakdown. Smoke filled the air as water soaked what was left of my apartment.

The fireman asked, "Is there anything you'd like to place in a storage ma'am?"

The fireman told us that tenants would receive free storage for a month. What was the point, I had nothing to save? My electronics, DVDs, and pictures were ruined. My son's framed photos were torn and wet. Camila convinced me to keep the twenty-four-inch square television and XBox 360 though they had water in them. She was convinced once they were dried, they would be able to work again.

The fireman followed me into the kitchen with a flashlight. The kitchen sink was filled with dirty dishes. I regretted not washing the dishes the previous night. I placed the dirty dishes in the trash. A jar of pennies I saved in my cupboard was missing. I looked around and noticed that most of the damage was caused by water rather than by fire. I had no property insurance; therefore, I was unable to get compensated or obtain coverage for property damage. The day of the fire I heard a woman say she canceled her insurance two days before the fire occurred. I knew she deeply regretted her decision.

The stench of smoke filled the bathroom and the shower curtain was burned and torn. Half of the bathroom ceiling was gone. I looked up to the ceiling and saw the blue sky. The day before the fire I had gone to a Family Dollar store and bought a new curtain, rug, and face towels. I left the bathroom and motioned to my son's room where I sat and cried. Camila opened my son's closet and held my son's baby outfit in her hand.

Camila said, "I thought this must be of value since you kept it."

I could barely say thank you.

I removed the SpongeBob window curtain along with the matching sheet and pillowcases. I placed everything in a large, black plastic bag together with a few toys my son often played with.

I entered my bedroom and saw my books on the bed soaked with water. I had books by Mary Monroe such as, *God Don't Like Ugly*, *God Don't Play*, and *God Ain't Blind*. I had not read or paid for the books. My mattress and clothes on the bed were soaked and reeked of smoke.

I saved my drenched, smoked clothing. I assumed the clothes could be washed and the stench of smoke would be removed.

Camila and I returned to the living room. A resident from my building entered my apartment and took pictures of my living room. The man said residents entered and stole items from victims' homes while the doors were left open at night. My jar of pennies and three fourteen karat gold wine glasses were missing. My living room was decorated in colors of gold, black and burgundy. Carla claimed her vacuum and other items were stolen.

Camila chuckled, "I heard a man walked out of someone's apartment early this morning with a plasma TV."

People had no remorse or respect for the victims. My heart sunk as I walked out of what used to be my home.

One afternoon I received a call from the secretary in the office at Plaza Village Apartments. The woman notified me of an apartment which was available and asked if I was interested. The woman explained that other clients refused the apartment since it was located in the basement. Why would a homeless person refuse an apartment? Of course I took the apartment. December 1st, I moved into a two-bedroom apartment in the plaza.

My new apartment was empty, yet I was grateful for a roof over my head. The apartment had heat, hot water, food, and utilities. I slept on an air mattress in my apartment that night. My son visited me that weekend and he was filled with excitement running through the rooms. We jumped on the air mattress like the air mattress was a trampoline.

No one got injured due to the fire; however residents lost valuable items. I heard that DCYF took the young boys from their parents. The only people who knew what happened were the parents.

God only gives us what we can bear. The church helped us keep our holiday spirit. The Redeemed Christian Church of God gave me a seven-foot-tall Christmas tree. A man who attended church in Warwick donated a bed, chair, microwave, and other items. What was surprising was that the man who was not looking for recognition gave me a four-hundred-dollar Walmart gift card. I did not expect this act of kindness from a stranger. There is a fire that burns in some people and warms the soul. That act of kindness made me the giving person I am today.

The fire was a blessing in disguise. When you ask God for things, it might not come when or how you expect it.

In the summer of 2011, I had mold in my bathroom. My son and I were sick. I complained to management; however the mold issue never got resolved. I wanted to move into a new apartment, but not that way. I am grateful for the apartment I moved into because it was bigger and better than the apartment I had before.

Years later, I was told that a man filmed the fire and posted the video on YouTube. I watched the video and saw that the man perceived the fire to be entertainment.

The man sang, "Fuego, Fuego" with a smile on his face. This man also shot a video of a girl being abused instead of helping.

In 2018, I spoke to the father of the two boys who was in building forty-one. The best person who would know what happened would be the people in the apartment where the fire started. The boys' father said that he returned home from doing laundry and his apartment was full of smoke. The mother of his children said that the boys were playing and knocked over a lamp, then the rug caught on fire. This story is different from what I have heard, though the fact remains, a fire occurred.

I had the biggest battle to fight, my battle with depression. Somewhere along life's journey I turned to prescription drugs for support. The next chapter is about my relationship with men. When it comes to men, I am totally clueless.

CHAPTER 22

# Totally Clueless

"Never make someone a priority
when all you are to them is an option."
— *Maya Angelou*

*E*very woman wants to find Mr. Right. Mr. Right for me would be someone attractive, sensitive, driven, confident, honest, and spiritual. He would have a sense of humor and stability in character. I believe a man with all those qualities only exists in fairytales.

A woman asked on her Facebook post, "if you were to describe your relationship based on a movie title, what would it be?" One woman answered, "Why did I get married?" My response would be "clueless" for I am totally clueless in regard to men.

I fell prey to the wrong men. I have dated men my age who wanted a mother rather than a girlfriend. I have learned that finding a date is similar to finding a job. You have to qualify, stand out, and leave a good impression. You have to offer men something they cannot get from someone else. A lady once asked me why such a beautiful girl like me was single. I answered that I am a homebody and do not meet many people. The woman asked how I can meet someone if no one knows a person like me exists. The woman referred me to a dating site called www. meetme.com.

I spoke to a man often on the dating site who claimed to be a medical assistant. I made the mistake of inviting the man into my home rather than meeting somewhere public. I am unfamiliar with the rules of dating. The man's wife called me the following day. I was unaware the man was married. The woman called me a slut and stated that she and the man had been married for six years. I explained that I was a single woman and her husband noted he was single on the dating site. The woman added, she knew where I lived since she tracked the GPS in the car. Something lacked in their marriage and the man was on the dating site looking for what was missing. What if the woman came to my home with a gun? I deleted the dating site app from my phone and decided to refrain from looking for men. I would let men find me. The wrong men found me in the spring of 2012.

Miguel, 44, a tall curly haired Puerto Rican, had moved to Woonsocket from New Jersey. We became friends; however, Miguel wanted a relationship rather than a friendship. Miguel said he was getting older and was ready to settle down.

Miguel spent the night during a snowstorm and refused to leave after the storm passed. I sent a text to Camilla from my bathroom stating I was using "Fleabag" to babysit as a joke. Miguel received the text meant for Camilla and I witnessed his temper. Miguel punched the bathroom door twice and shouted that he would punch me very hard in the jaw and that I would be drinking out of a straw for six months. I locked myself inside the bathroom and opened the door when I heard my exterior door slam. My biggest regret was welcoming Miguel's return.

Miguel came back to my home later to inform me his mother was ill and he needed to return to New Jersey. Miguel complained of being unable to afford storage and that he had to take his furniture with him.

My furniture endured vast amounts of water damage due to

the fire in my building. Miguel needed money and storage and I needed furniture; therefore, I offered to buy his furniture. The furniture consisted of a hunter green suede couch and a loveseat recliner. Miguel also added a burgundy and green rug which complemented the furniture. Miguel sold the furniture to me for the price of two hundred and fifty dollars. The price he asked for the furniture was unbelievable. I wrote the arrangement on paper then we went to the library to notarize the agreement. Miguel said the money would be used to buy a bus ticket to New Jersey.

Miguel refused to leave and made excuses as to why. Miguel explained he needed to leave with clean clothes. I washed Miguel's laundry and found a paper with a telephone number in the pants pocket of his jeans. I called the number from the laundry room and a woman from Ohio answered. The woman told me of domestic and animal abuse. Miguel broke a bird's neck in front of a child. The woman said that a warrant was issued for Miguel's arrest in the state of Ohio. I wondered not who, but what did I bring into my home? I harbored a fugitive. I conducted my own investigation online and saw that Miguel had minor criminal charges.

I called the police department to inform them of Miguel and the department failed to take action. Miguel confirmed the information I had when I confronted him.

One afternoon, Miguel entered my apartment and two pair of underwear fell out of his pants pocket.

Miguel said, "I don't need you; I can have any five-dollar hoe."

I refused to have sex with Miguel and he forced himself on me.

According to my diary, on February 23rd, 2012, I leaned over the kitchen sink to wash dishes. Miguel leaned against me, pulled my pants down, and said he was taking his money. Miguel added, his furniture cost thousands of dollars. I picked up a knife from the kitchen sink.

Miguel shouted, "I will knock you out with a punch before you could swing that knife!"

I managed to escape from Miguel's grasp and told him he would receive the fifty dollars I owed him. I purposely withheld fifty dollars from Miguel for using my closet to store women's undergarments. Miguel insisted that even though I gave him the money, he would not leave until the second of March.

On February 24th, I spoke with a sergeant at the police station about my experience with Miguel.

Sergeant Burns said, "You could come to file a complaint in the office, but you will have to file a restraining order at court."

Sergeant Burns suggested I should change the locks on my door. I told him that my landlord said the cost to change the locks on my door is one hundred dollars.

The female officer, Sergeant Burns, said, "Nothing in this world is free ma'am."

The officer explained what would happen when I filed a restraining order. The officer said if Miguel was absent from court, the case would be dismissed. She added, the restraining order would be canceled.

My landlord agreed to have my locks changed at one o'clock that afternoon. I went to the police station to file a complaint after my locks were changed.

I arrived at the police station and spoke to a female officer. The officer failed to file a complaint. The officer said that what she would do is document that I have contacted the police numerous times to remove Miguel from my apartment. The officer added that Miguel could get arrested for trespassing. She suggested I file a no contact order and refrain from contacting Miguel. On March 2nd, I received numerous phone calls from Miguel.

"It's me you stupid bitch!" Miguel shouted repeatedly.

Miguel sent me a picture of him and a white woman when I ended the call. Miguel texted that he would make me lose my son, and that he placed cocaine inside the couch and had contacted child protective services. I felt sick and vomited in the toilet.

I became depressed and discussed my situation with my psychiatrist. My psychiatrist called the rescue for me and I was admitted to the hospital. I participated in group therapy at the hospital and was discharged after seventy-two hours with a treatment plan. As part of the treatment plan, I had to continue therapy and medication.

On February 17th, I started outpatient therapy and met with a team at Community Care Alliance. I saw a therapist every two weeks, a psychiatrist every three months, a caseworker and a vocational worker.

About two months later, I met a man named Loyd. Loyd in his late forties, was tall, dark and friendly. Loyd's mother died and he had recently moved to Woonsocket. I met Loyd at a neighbor's house while I searched for a phone charger. I was still receiving threatening messages from Miguel. Loyd saw I was upset and invited me to his home to talk while I charged my phone. Loyd spoke of his failed marriage and childhood. My problems were minor compared to Loyd's.

Loyd invited me over to his apartment one night since I had difficulty sleeping. I laid on Loyd's couch to watch television and took my medication which made me constipated. Loyd gave me a laxative to take with my medication and that was the last thing I remembered. I woke up naked in Loyd's bed the following morning.

Loyd had a huge smile on his face and said, "Last night was amazing, you gave your all to me last night."

I had no recollection of how I got into Loyd's bed. I told Loyd I had no memory of anything.

Loyd was annoyed and angry, "Well I'm no rapist; we had sex last night!"

I accused Loyd of giving me drugs. I left Loyd's apartment and went to Camilla's apartment. I called the pharmacy from Camilla's and explained what happened. The pharmacist suggested

I do a drug screen. I went to the pharmacy and the pharmacist performed a urinary drug screen to detect substances. The only drugs in my system were my prescription drugs and the laxative Loyd gave me. I felt I had to apologize to Loyd for the accusation; however, Camilla thought Loyd took advantage of me. I wanted an explanation as to why I forgot the whole night.

I spoke to my psychiatrist about my medications during an appointment. My doctor said that one of the side effects of Ambien is that it can cause amnesia. My psychiatrist discontinued the Ambien and prescribed me Trazodone to sleep. According to my medication log, On May 21st, I started 25 milligrams of Atarax Hydroxyzine, 50 milligrams of Trazodone, and 40 milligrams of Paxil Paroxetine. I am unaware of when I started Ambien since Plaza Psychology only keeps records for five years.

I apologized to Loyd for the accusation despite Camilla's disapproval. Loyd was extremely talented. Loyd played guitar, carved eagle sculptures, and he was an artist. Loyd had dreams, ambition, but no drive. Loyd was also a professional liar. Men who cheat are referred to as dogs; however, I disagree. Dogs are loyal. A woman cannot tame or place a man on a tight leash. A woman could give a man the stars, yet that will not be enough to keep that man. The only thing that will keep a man is a man who wants to be kept. I expected more from a man who was honest about his infidelity from the beginning. Loyd confessed he cheated on his ex-wife with her best friend when we met. As a result, Loyd's ex-wife tried to poison him by placing boric acid in his food.

Loyd introduced me to his friends and we formed a group. We called the group "The NRI Club." We were neighbors who sought help from the same non-profit organization called Community Care Alliance of Northern Rhode Island. This organization helps individuals with mental illness, addiction, housing issues, employment, and other needs.

We gathered at Earl's apartment to watch Tyler Perry movies or Lifetime. Earl, one of Loyd's friends, was a frail, white man with Parkinson's disease. Loyd and I built a birdhouse which we placed outside Earl's window. Earl was down to earth, friendly, and loved birds, yet he struggled with alcohol. Earl would curse you today and say he loved you the next day. I was the youngest in the group and had to get used to Loyd's friends. We had our struggles, but laughter was the best medicine when we were unable to rely on prescribed medications. Loyd was convinced he wanted a relationship with me and gave me his social security number and date of birth. I had to be certain he was safe considering my experience with Miguel. Miguel was escorted out of my building, yet he roamed the streets. I was unable to show comparison between Loyd and Miguel as they both proved age is just a number. My son at the age of eight told Loyd he should act his age and not his shoe size.

I called Loyd's house phone one day and Loyd's son's mother answered the phone. I had an attitude and hung up the phone while she was talking. This violent woman left Loyd's apartment then came to Earl's apartment and assaulted me in front of my son. My son is 14 and is still unable to get this image out of his head today. The woman was old enough to be my mother. Loyd acted as a referee, appearing to be entertained by the drama. I saw Loyd kiss a white woman outside one day and I approached him about it.

Loyd exclaimed, "You're hallucinating; you need to check your meds!"

The medications I consumed were not at fault. Camilla and I stood on the stairs and saw Loyd kiss the woman through the window. Loyd brought me sexual gratification, probably the only reason I tried to hold on to him.

I wondered if Loyd could be tamed. I pretended to have menstruation to avoid having sex with unfaithful Loyd. Loyd disliked rejection and when I rejected Loyd, I sent him into the arms of another woman. A woman called to inform me Loyd spent the night at her house. The woman said she saw my telephone number on the television screen when I called his house phone.

The woman explained that she and Loyd were having sex; therefore, he ignored the phone. I heard Loyd's voice in the background when the woman was on the phone with me. I decided to punish Loyd. Loyd was allergic to onions and that is exactly what I cooked with when I invited him over for dinner.

Loyd spoke negatively of the woman he was with. Loyd said that the woman was unable to cook, that she burned water. Nobody is perfect and if he spoke ill of her, I wondered what he said about me.

On the 16th of June, I felt suicidal and called the emergency line at Community Care Alliance. I had other stressors besides the unhealthy relationship with Loyd. I was unemployed, had no family support, and being a full-time mother was overwhelming. The day Loyd's daughter and girlfriend fought me; I had reached my breaking point. I spoke to a woman on the emergency line and she called the rescue for me. I needed to escape from my problems. Women's problems do start with men such as: **MEN**struation, **MEN**opause, and **MEN**tal illness just to name a few. I believed I got involved with boys instead of men. I have dated boys mistaken for men despite their age.

In 2014, Earl died and so did our support group, NRI Club. I felt as though a family member died. I believed the birds felt Earl's absence since they ceased to enter the yard. Earl loved and always fed the birds. The place felt like a dead zone when Earl died. Everyone in our group departed and Loyd moved out of his apartment. I remained in my apartment, though I had to stop myself when I realized I was walking to Earl's apartment.

I continued to see a therapist every two weeks. My therapist joked that I should take a vacation from men.

To conclude, I believe my poor judgement and bad choice in men was the cause for my unfulfilled relationships. I should have had my parents growing up to teach me the "scoop" on men. I was in need of a book called *Men for Dummies* or *The Idiot's Guide to Learning About Men* if such books exist.

A few years later, in 2017, I stumbled upon a book at the

library called *Love Smart* by Dr. Phillip C. McGraw, Ph.D. Dr. Phil's book could have saved me had I discovered it in 2012. In his book, on page 74, Dr. Phil said, "You teach people how to treat you."

Maybe unintentionally, I did in fact teach those men how to treat me. I sent the wrong message and failed to demand respect. Now I am not desperate to find a mate like I was desperate to find a job; willing to accept anything available. I decided to focus on me rather than making men a priority. I was unsure of the qualities I had to offer.

I continued my medications assuming they would make me feel better. Javier, my son's father, feared the medications would do more harm than good. Javier questioned my choice in men and felt his child was unsafe with me. Javier wanted sole custody even if he had to accuse me of assault to build a case against me. So in the year 2013, I was charged with assault.

# CHAPTER 23

# The Assault Charge

"No one has power over you unless you
give it to them. You are in control of your life
and your choices, decide your own fate."
— *Leon Brown, baseball player*

In 2013, Javier and I had gone to court for mediation. Javier expressed to the mediator that he wanted custody of our son. Javier explained that he feared the medications I consumed would do more harm than good. The woman responded that the judge would not remove my son from my custody for taking medications. The woman added that the judge would view me as a mother who was trying to help herself. Javier was disappointed when my son remained in my custody.

One afternoon, my son repeatedly knocked his head on the wall. I am unsure as to whether his action was out of boredom or whether he craved attention. I was unable to control or discipline my son so, I called Javier to ask for help. Javier neglected to help me, and instead he called the police. Javier made known to the police that he feared for the safety of his child.

The policeman entered my apartment and scanned my walls with his eyes. What was he expecting to find? The walls of my apartment were bare without a punch hole or a frame on the wall. The male officer spoke to my son in private. The officer informed me he was performing an investigation due to a phone call he received from my son's father.

On another dreadful day, I left my son with a neighbor while I went to do errands. The woman's son had soccer practice; therefore, she warned me to return in a hurry. I stayed at the store longer than intended. I went to retrieve my son and the woman said that since she was late for her son's soccer practice,, she gave my son to his father. The woman said that she saw Javier walking and she drove Javier home with my son.

Earl's girlfriend drove me to Javier's parents' house to retrieve my son. I heard laughter and sounds from inside the house. I knocked on the door but no one answered. I called the house phone and failed to get a response. Everyone at the table ignored the door and phone. I returned home without my son enraged. Javier informed me once, whenever the house phone rings, his family knows I am the one calling since they have cellular phones. I was being ignored. I was frustrated and called Javier's parents' house at ten p.m. Javier answered the phone and he told me that I left my son unattended. Javier threatened to alert the DCYF. Javier said he would take our son to school in the morning. Javier made life difficult for me rather than to help me.

I walked to my son's school one afternoon enraged. I knew Javier would be at the school. I approached Javier, shoved my finger in his face, yelled and cursed him. Parents outside watched in shock as I humiliated Javier.

I returned home and not too long after, I heard a loud knock on the door. I opened it and a male and female officer stood at the front door. I pretended to be confused as to why they were there. I knew Javier called the police on me. The officers verified my identity and arrested me without being mirandized. I panicked and denied I laid a hand on Javier.

Javier informed the police that I slapped him across the face. I spoke to the officers about Javier and my relationship. The officers commented that they often see cases like this when there is a custody battle. Neighbors watched as I entered the police car.

On September 26th, 2012, I was charged with domestic assault. The officers took my photograph and fingerprints when I arrived at the station. I was in a jail cell for two hours and my anxiety increased. I was alone in the cell and reached out to family members. I called my sister Audrica and asked her to bail me out. My sister said she used all her money to bail out our brother Andrew. Andrew was my oldest brother, referred to as Jailbird since he was in jail often.

My last desperate call was made to Kevin. Kevin was on his way to the men's shelter in Providence when I called. Kevin had to be at the shelter before seven p.m. in order to receive a bed. Kevin was in disbelief when I spoke of my situation and refused to remain in the city. I pleaded with Kevin to reconsider his decision. I offered to return the money he would use to bail me out of jail the following day. Kevin hesitated, though he agreed to return to Woonsocket to pay for my release.

Kevin helped me; however, he had no place to sleep for the night. Kevin would have slept at the men's shelter had I not begged him to place my bail. Kevin wanted to sleep in his truck that night, but I insisted he come to my apartment. Kevin had Chronic Obstructive Pulmonary Disease (COPD) and no heat in his truck. The New England weather is unstable in the fall. The temperature is hot during the day and drops to numbing cold at night. My son says the weather is bipolar. I allowed Kevin to sleep in my room and I slept on the couch. Unlike most people, I am most comfortable on my couch.

The following morning I gave Kevin the money he spent for my release from jail. Kevin said that Adrienne saw his truck packed in the parking lot overnight and reported to my mother at the nursing home that we had slept together. I had now alienated myself even more from my family.

On February 25th, the case of domestic assault was dismissed in court. I had a public defender and my therapist accompanied me for support. Javier was unable to maintain his story in court. At the school, Javier complained to the police officers that I slapped him across his face. The police officer took the stand and testified, upon arrival at the elementary school, he saw no visible bruises on Javier's face. Javier stood and the judge asked him where I hit him.

Javier said, "I believed she poked me your honor."

Which is it? Did I slap you or did I poke you? Javier had no witness for his false accusation.

The judge ordered me to enroll in anger management classes and to continue therapy. Indeed, I needed anger management classes because I wanted to slap Javier.

On April 5th, the assault charge was expunged. Javier continued to be a pain in my existence until I accepted his behavior. I gave up.

CHAPTER 24

# Accused of Larceny

It was September 26th, and I felt suicidal. I called the Community Care Alliance to express concerns for my safety. The ambulance came and transported me to the hospital. The nurse extracted six vials of blood from me at the hospital and requested a urine sample. To my astonishment, my urine tested positive for crack.

I called my caseworker the next morning to complain about my urine test results. I had never held a cigarette in my life. I was upset upon arrival at the hospital and the nurse gave me a pill called Valium to help me relax. I assumed the pill was the cause for my urinalysis. I spoke to a patient at the hospital and the patient explained that the urine test must be a false-positive. The patient told me that some drugs do not interact well with other antidepressants. I found the revelation to be absurd. Later I was informed I had to be admitted to the acute stabilization unit (ASU).

On September 27th, I was admitted at the ASU. The Acute Stabilization Unit is a step-down unit for adults experiencing psychiatric and substance abuse related crises. I did not belong in this place.

I participated in peer support groups and therapy groups at the unit. I engaged in art, music, and exercise which were part of the treatment plan. In the art group, I colored and made necklaces with my son's name on them, and in the music group the staff played songs to help with depression. The staff played the song, "Hold On" by Wilson Phillips, one of the few I remembered. Although patients felt better than when they arrived, this unit was not the place to make friends.

We humans create our own problems sometimes. I discovered ways to improve my mood at the unit. I befriended a patient named Howard. Howard, a tall, white Caucasian male was cheerful and had an uplifting spirit. The staff was surprised at how overjoyed he was when everyone was down. Howard's happiness in the morning was an insult to the rest of us patients. Howard made me laugh, something I had not done in a long time.

On October 2nd, I was discharged from the unit. I presumed I would never see Howard again until I saw him a few weeks later. I was in Kevin's blue truck when I saw Howard with a suitcase he was dragging behind him. I asked Kevin to stop the truck. Howard said he needed a place to stay temporarily since his father kicked him out of the house.

I took a risk and brought Howard to my home. Howard was supposed to stay for a few days. My son was with his father for a few days and I made choices I regret. I smoked marijuana with Howard and his friend. Howard commented that he could tell I never smoked from the way I held my lighter and cigarette. I wanted to do something I never did to experience something different. I realized smoking was not a habit I would adapt to.

I took my son one day to the GameStop after school, then we returned home.

My son entered the house and asked with a teary voice, "Mommy where's the TV?"

The fifty-five-inch plasma LG television I rented from a furniture store was gone. My Xbox 360 game system was also missing. I called the police to file a report. The police suggested I contact local pawn shops to learn if anything had been pawned recently. I called the pawn shops; however, no game system or television had been pawned. The neighbor upstairs told me that she saw two boys with a large, black garbage bag run out of my apartment. At the mention of two boys, I knew Howard and his friend stole from me. I cleaned my apartment and found Howard's identification card on the living room rug. The amateur thief must have dropped his identification card when he ran out of my apartment. I wrote Howard's ID information on a paper and brought the paper to the furniture store where I rented the television from.

The manager shouted, "You know who has my TV? Then go get it!"

The manager threatened to take legal action and spoke of extra fines. I paid over nine hundred dollars to rent the television; however, I still owed money. The manager at the furniture store believed I intentionally stole from them. The manager was right about one thing: I was responsible for their belongings. This was the price I paid for bringing strangers into my home.

I endured an unpleasant experience; however, I took full responsibility. What would I have done differently? I would refrain from inviting a stranger into my home; especially a man I met at a substance abuse unit. Howard and his friend stole more than just material things from me. Howard and his partner in crime stole my time, energy, and respect for humanity.

This experience has taught me that you can be kind; however, you cannot allow people to abuse you.

In 2013, I lost material things that could be replaced. In 2015, a cry for help led me to lose everything that mattered and was irreplaceable.

# CHAPTER 25

# A Cry for Help

*"Up from a past that's rooted in pain I rise."*
*— Maya Angelou; American poet,*
*memoirist and a voice for women.*

On August 11ᵗʰ, 2015, I felt suicidal. I took a knife from the kitchen with intentions to harm myself. I called my caseworker at NRI and asked her to take my son. I was overwhelmed and in the wrong state of mind to care for my son. My caseworker Jessica came and called the rescue for me to be admitted to the hospital.

I met with Doctor Louis in the mental health unit at Saint Rita's hospital. Doctor Louis presumed the prescription drugs I consumed caused my suicidal thoughts and as a result he altered my prescriptions. Doctor Louis discontinued the Klonopin and Paxil that I started in 2013. Klonopin and Paxil were prescribed to help me with my depression and anxiety. The doctor said he discontinued my medications to prevent me from being on two narcotic drugs at once. Doctor Louis increased my dosage of Wellbutrin from seventy-five to one hundred and fifty milligrams. The doctor explained that my weight was the reason he increased the dose of my prescription. I weighed one hundred and forty-eight pounds at the age of thirty-two. The doctor said it will be difficult, but I will live.

The alteration of my prescriptions caused my health to decline. I experienced symptoms of sciatica in my hip and leg. I was deprived of sleep, stuttered, and trembled uncontrollably. My health insurance covered my stay at the hospital for a short time, though I needed more care. I was released from the hospital on the nineteenth of August.

The doctor gave me prescriptions to refill after I was discharged from the hospital. The pharmacist looked at me as I trembled in front of her. The pharmacist explained that he believed my prescribed dosage was too high. The pharmacist refused to refill the prescriptions and suggested I consult with my doctor to adjust my medications. I resembled a junkie in need of a fix. I arrived at Community Care Alliance and I stood at the front of the receptionist desk. I struggled to speak. The receptionist called the nurse immediately. The nurse wanted to have me admitted to the CSU however, beds were unavailable. I could have died. I wanted to pursue legal action against the hospital, but my therapist was against the idea. I just thanked God I was alive.

The ambulance took me to another hospital other than Saint Rita's. I was admitted at the hospital to verify if I had sciatica and to have medications adjusted. My medications were adjusted and my stuttering and trembling slowed. I tested negative for sciatica, still, the doctor suggested I attend physical therapy after my discharge. The doctor prescribed me new medications to see if my mental health would improve. I was scared of the side effects of the new drugs and on October 16th, 2015, I made a difficult decision.

Javier and I were requested at court. Javier arrived with his parents and I was alone. I paced back and forth from the courtroom to the restroom. I was nervous to make this life changing decision. I had to decide whether I should allow my son to stay in temporary foster care or give placement to my son's grandparents who detested me. My mother was not an option as she was in a nursing home and my father was in another country. I needed to take care of my mental and physical health. Was I selfish? How can a mother take care of a child if she needs to care for herself? I signed a motion giving consent to Javier's parents to have placement of my son while Javier and I have joint custody.

Javier tried to deceive me in my fragile state of mind. Javier tried to persuade me to give his parents physical custody. I failed to write what Javier wanted. Javier tried to convince me that physical custody and placement was the same thing. Placement is who the child lives with, but a person with custody has all the authority and can even migrate with the child. I agreed to placement as I believed was the best decision at the time. I was at the mental health unit often and being a full-time mother was difficult. I hesitated while approaching the judge.

Javier's mother, Teressa, said that I would be able to see my son at any time. I was unaware I was to be alienated from my son.

My son had a doctor's appointment I wanted to take him to, yet Teressa insisted on taking him to this appointment. My son's appointment was to check his cholesterol and insulin levels. Teressa suggested I rest while she took my son to this appointment and I agreed. Teressa discovered at my son's appointment that his cholesterol and insulin levels had increased. Teressa embedded in my son's head that I made him sick and that I did not deserve him.

My son cried for two weeks to return home. My son missed his friend, his room, and his mother. Teressa denied all reasonable requests for visitation besides every other weekend. I was forbidden to see my son on birthdays, holidays, school vacations, Mother's Day and even major holidays like Thanksgiving and Christmas.

I walked towards my son after school one day to hug him and Teressa pulled him away. It was a pain that felt worse than sciatica. My house was not a home anymore and I felt empty without him. I called Teressa and asked to spend time with my son; however, she suggested I should return to court to obtain visitation.

October 27th, I spoke with a lawyer, Mr. Franklyn Barrett. Mr. Barrett said that the judge should never have signed the document because the document was written incorrectly. The lawyer also questioned my mental and physical state when I signed the document.

November 16th,, my lawyer interviewed me. I filled out paperwork to waive the filing fee then we drove to the courthouse. The clerk at the courthouse asked for income verification. My lawyer took me to retrieve my award letter from the social security office then we returned to the courthouse.

The day was long and disappointing. My lawyer and I went to room 3B to see Judge Roberts. Honorable Judge Roberts at the family court was not thrilled to see my lawyer and me.

Judge Roberts' voice was harsh and loud. "Get out of my courtroom. I do not want to see your face again!"

My lawyer walked away revealing no emotion.

Judge Roberts' looked at me and shouted, "You're near poverty and you brought a lawyer?!"

I was embarrassed. I motioned to exit the courtroom and said under my breath, "Thanks for nothing."

Judge Roberts must have heard what I said and he ordered the police officer to lock me in a cell. I had to return to room 3B at 4:30 p.m. to apologize to the judge. I cried. I stayed in the cell for four hours wishing I had given this contemptible judge a piece of my mind. I was infuriated. I wanted the judge to know he was not God, but a man in uniform. God must have been tired when he created him for he was ugly. My lawyer sympathized with me and offered to take me home. Fortunately, I saw my lawyer before he went home.

"They told me you left already," My lawyer added.

My lawyer dropped me home at seven that evening.

I begged Teressa for months to allow me to spend extra time

with my son and she denied me. All I could do was write about it in my diary.

November 20th, I again asked Teressa for my son and she responded negatively.

Teressa said, "No, the court paper doesn't state you can spend extra time with him."

I said, "The court paper also did not give you permission to travel to another state with my son, but you did."

Teressa suggested we should return to court and I agreed. I missed my son, he gave me a purpose, a reason to live. I missed those morning hugs, good night kisses, his laughter and his presence. But on December 5th,, I pleaded again and got the same response.

Teressa replied, "Enrique is in karate every day. His dad wants him to take karate on Saturdays as well. If you want to see him, get a court order."

I was uninformed of any decision regarding school activities and events. I was excluded from my son's daily life. I spent Thanksgiving and Christmas alone. But I avoided having another breakdown and getting admitted to the hospital.

February 26th, I received a call from my lawyer. My lawyer advised against attending court as he failed to hear from the sheriff. Mr. Franklyn Barrett wanted to discuss another court date and fees. I gave my lawyer three hundred and fifty dollars and failed to have a court date. My lawyer made known he had superior cases.

July 15th, I arrived at court to modify the visitation agreement and regain placement of my son. My therapist accompanied me for moral support. My dumb lawyer failed to do the basic thing like notify the judge that his client was present at court. My case was dismissed due to my lawyer's indiscretion. My lawyer felt intimidated by my therapist presence and left for a long coffee and cigarette break. My therapist used two words to describe my lawyer: unprofessional and incompetent. I was furious and threw my phone across the courtroom in frustration.

Javier, his mother, and my son were present at court; however, they left as they assumed I was not present.

I decided to be strong and changed my circumstance. I was exhausted from pleading for my son and calling this Spanish lady Teressa *puta*. I obtained employment at a nursing home as a certified nursing assistant. I worked three days a week from three in the afternoon to eleven at night. Transportation expenses were costly since I took a taxi to and from work.

Teressa demanded child support from me.

Teressa said, "My son was paying seventy-five dollars a week so I want seventy-five dollars a week."

I gave Teressa no money in the beginning, then I realized if my son were to live with me, I would have to pay for a babysitter. My therapist suggested I give Teressa money in the form of a money order in order to keep the receipts. I opened a child savings account for my son at the Milford Federal Bank and bought my son what he needed. I made the best out of the six days a month I spent with my son. We went to the Providence Mall and the movies often. My son said that if I were to work in the morning he would return home. A wise idea indeed; however, as a new employee, the only shift available to me was second shift, three to eleven. First shift, seven in the morning to three in the afternoon was in high demand. My employer suggested I write a written request for the first shift. But the first shift never became available.

Teressa tried to convince me that my son did not care for me.

One day my son said to me, "Mom, every day with you is like Christmas."

Everyone knows how a child looks forward to the joy of Christmas.

> Did you want to see me broken?
> Bowed head and lowered eyes?
> Shoulders falling down like teardrops?
> Weakened by my soulful cries?
> *— From Maya Angelou poem, 'Still I Rise.' 1928-2014*

CHAPTER 26

# My Battle with Depression

"Never bend your head, always hold it high.
Look the world straight in the eye."
– *Helen Keller; American author, first deaf and
blind person to earn a bachelor of arts degree.*

*W*hen I lost the opportunity to regain placement of my son, I swore I lost my mind. My therapist suggested I join a writing or an art group. I joined a group called the "Frolicking Goddess Craft Studio." The group leader was a talented lady who taught individuals how to crochet, knit, bead, and do embroidery. She also taught members of the group how to make bags from worn out clothing. I was interested in beading and made jewelry with crystals which had healing benefits. One of my favorite crystals was amethyst. I researched the benefits of amethyst and learned that the crystal was known to alleviate sadness and physical pain. I beaded with magnets, rose quartz, tiger eye, and evil eye beads. The experience was resourceful and therapeutic.

My job, the climate, and my personal life created stress and affected my mental and physical health. I took a great risk and discontinued prescription drugs such as Atarax, Seroquel, Trazodone and replaced them with Melatonin. I consumed whole food vitamins, fish oil, and a vitamin C supplement. My mood improved and I felt more motivated. I even became a gym member at Planet Fitness. Who needs a pill when you could run on a treadmill? I lost ten pounds and felt a sense of accomplishment. My son noticed the change and made healthy changes in his life as well. My son's grades and health improved. My son's physical exercise, the karate, was the reason for the change, though Teressa took credit. My son was happy and spoke of his abuelo (grandfather) often. My heart was broken he was no longer in my care, yet he was happy and I was happy for him. I tried to look at my situation in a positive way. I cared for myself while my son was with his grandparents.

The first thing I did was I learn to say no. This small word no is such a difficult word to say. Most of the situations I was in could have been avoided if only I said no. No to recurring ex-boyfriends, stressful jobs, and anything I disliked. I resigned from my stressful nursing assistant job. My anxiety increased there and I worked extra shifts thus causing me to lose focus. I decided to make the best out of the time and opportunity I had.

October 28th, 2016, I spoke with my vocational worker Brian at NRI about furthering my education. My goal was to enroll at the Community College of Rhode Island in the spring semester; however, I missed the deadline to register in August. The administrator suggested I wait to register for the fall semester in January of 2017. I was interested in the registered nurse degree program. The goal of attending college was placed on hold when I discovered I had a defaulted loan. I had to make a payment arrangement plan with the loan company. I had set no limitations.

That year I did things I never imagined I could do. I braided my own hair when someone said no to me, I made jewelry, and I lost weight. I was diagnosed with major depression, anxiety, post-traumatic stress disorder, and mood disorder. Some days were difficult to rise from bed as though an invisible force pulled me down. I realized that life is stress and the way to survive is by taking control.

The following year, 2017, a certain situation placed me in a position where I was unable to take control. I had a breakdown and lost my battle with depression.

What broke me that year were numerous grievances, everyday stress, and failed attempts of having a life. I was trapped in an unwanted life. A life without my son, unemployment, unpaid debts, and one disappointment after another. I wanted my son to live with me, have a career, earn a degree in journalism or nursing, and to handle life. I pursued the same nursing assistant jobs which were stressful. I obtained a job at a nursing home as a nursing assistant in April 2017 and resigned in July of that year. I dealt with combative residents, overwhelmed myself with extra shifts, and got drained. I resigned over the phone which I admit was an unprofessional way to leave a job.

The decision was both a relief and a burden. I was relieved I could care for myself; however, the fact I resigned caused a financial burden. I received four hundred and fifty-eight dollars once a month from the Social Security Administration. I received that amount weekly when I had a weekly steady income. I received a letter from the social security office stating that my monthly gross income increased when I worked; therefore, my income would be two dollars for the month of December. Two dollars? What can I do with two dollars? A cheeseburger from McDonalds cost two dollars and forty-seven cents. I felt as though I was being punished for trying to be financially independent.

I searched for a job at an independent living facility. I was scheduled to start the weekend my son visited. The nurse advised me to call to see if someone would be willing to switch weekends with me. The following Monday I called the facility in the presence of my vocational worker. In a rude tone of voice, the woman answered negatively and hung up the phone. My vocational worker and I looked at each other in bewilderment. I felt discouraged and ceased to look for work. I planned on furthering my education to obtain a better job.

I went to Community College of Rhode Island with my

vocational worker to apply for financial aid. The financial aid advisor mentioned that I needed to remove my loans from default from Lincoln Technical Institute in order to qualify for financial aid. The advisor informed me that a few classes would cost six hundred dollars which excluded textbooks. I called to make a payment arrangement plan with the loan company; however, I would have to pay the interest before I paid the principal loan. I filed my taxes and the Internal Revenue Service garnished my wages to pay some of my student loan debt. The entire nine hundred and sixty-seven dollars was paid to the Department of Education. I had little food in my apartment and seventeen cents in my account. A co-worker, Mohammed, gave me fifty dollars to buy food for my son when he visited.

My son accidentally knocked the shelves off my bathroom wall when he visited one day. He rushed to get prepared to go karate with his grandmother. I wanted to patch the holes in the wall and hang the shelves when my son left for karate. I needed drywall repair putty and regretted asking Loyd's friend Clyde. When you want something done, the best thing is to do it yourself. You will save yourself a headache and heartache. Clyde gave the putty to Loyd to bring to me. I assumed Loyd would deliver the items and leave; however, he offered to help repair the wall and hang the shelves. He spoke of his construction experience and stated he would do a better job than I could. I rejected Loyd's offer, yet he was persistent. I relented and warned that Loyd should leave before my son returned from karate. I made known I wanted to avoid any confrontation with his girlfriend. Loyd told me he had plenty of time to help since he expected his girlfriend at nine. As we worked on the shelves we flirted, and flirting led to oral sex in the room. Loyd left around seven, leaving a beer, cigarette, putty, and paint behind. Loyd left through my back door and my son entered through the front. My son brought his friend to play video games in the living room.

I heard a loud knock on the window. Loyd's girlfriend was outside yelling for me to come outside in an angry tone of voice.

I assumed she wanted to fight and I ignored her. Sharon, Loyd's girlfriend, had gotten out of work sooner than Loyd expected. I should have called the police to report a disturbance though Sharon eventually left.

The following Thursday night I was with Rafael. Rafael was someone I was intimate with over the summer. He slept over my apartment that Thursday night.

Friday afternoon Rafael appeared to be asleep and I arose from bed to cook. I had chicken with vegetables in the oven and rice on the stove. I played reggaeton "Barcito Despacito" in the kitchen.

I heard a knock on my door and asked who was there. Loyd made known he was at the door. I assumed Loyd came for the items he left at my house. I tried to spy into the peep hole in the door when Sharon kicked it open. Loyd and Sharon forced their way in my apartment as I tried to push my door closed. My cry for help was left unanswered. Sharon assaulted me and Loyd blocked all attempts for me to defend myself. The police would have been at my apartment within minutes had I not uninstalled the security alarm.

I ran into the bathroom and tried to close the door, but Sharon followed me. Loyd stood at the front of me as I tried to hit Sharon with a shelf from the bathroom. They both left after I cried for Loyd to get Sharon out of my apartment. Sharon left the evidence of her crime behind. Sharon left her phone, one slipper, an earring, and a twenty-dollar bill.

I motioned to the living room and sat on the couch wounded with disappointments. Rafael, a sorry excuse for a man, came into sight.

Rafael uttered, "I called the cops they're on their way. Are you okay? I was going to hit him with the guitar you had in your closet."

Rafael explained that he suffered from anxiety due to a bad experience and he had to leave for work. Rafael left my apartment and I texted Camila about what happened. Camila commented that I had a pussy for a boyfriend. She texted, "what kind of a man would stay to watch a girl get beat up and not do anything about it."

The truth is people have the right to be how they are whether or not they meet our expectations. I was disappointed since I expected more from Rafael. He asked if I had slept with Loyd. Maybe he felt I deserved to get assaulted.

Two policemen arrived at my home, officers Paul and Jean. The officers took my statement and wrote a report. I tried to show the officers visible bruises; however, the officer was distracted from what he was writing. One officer asked me to adjust the volume on the radio and I turned it off. I reported what had happened. The officers were more interested in why Rafael neglected to help and why he left before they arrived. The officers requested Rafael's full name and informed me that Rafael had a prior incident with domestic assault on his ex-girlfriend. The officers assumed that Rafael was the one who assaulted me. He might as well have assaulted me. There are two kinds of bad people in this world; people who do bad things and people who see bad things happening and do nothing to stop them.

I kept the twenty-dollar bill and gave the officers Sharon's phone as evidence. I discarded the slipper and earring Sharon left in the bathroom.

The officers told me that I should request a report to take to court the following Monday, file a restraining order, and press charges. Sharon avoided arrest as she was nowhere to be found.

Monday I called the station and a female dispatcher answered the phone.

The female dispatcher sounded aggravated. "Stop calling, you called twelve times. I have other people calling. When you call, instead of pressing nine, press four. I don't want to hear your story."

Sergeant Manning was the detective who worked on my case. I was anxious to know why they neglected to make an arrest. To make matters worse, my sister's boyfriend knocked on my door.

He mentioned my sister wanted to know if I was okay because she heard I got stabbed. I felt as though my sister was too late to be concerned about me. She lives in the same building as me yet we had not spoken in years.

My past flooded through my mind. I wondered if I could make all this hurt, pain, and guilt go away. Negative thoughts rummaged through my head. I tried to hide my tears, and on August ninth, I again contemplated suicide. I had a specific plan to slash my wrist in a tub of cold water. Who would miss me? I felt my son did great without me. I had no motivation to live. I tried to remember what I learned from group therapy at the mental health unit. I remembered uplifting songs. The song "Lullaby" by Nickelback helped me refrain from that decision. I guess I needed to hear positive words in a dark time.

That day I spoke to the nurse at NRI. I refused to be hospitalized; however, I wanted to vent since I expected my son that weekend. The nurse was skeptical about my safety at home and I was admitted to Saint Claire's Hospital.

At the hospital a girl accompanied my roommate and I to our lunch table. The girl placed a book on the table titled, *You Are a Badass* and said that this self-help book helped her. I wrote the title of the book on a piece of paper as a reminder to buy the book later.

On August 15th, I waited to be discharged from the mental health unit at Saint Claire's Hospital. The psychiatrist requested to see me in his office before I left. The doctor said I was not being treated for what I have which is Bipolar disorder. The psychiatrist prescribed me 600 milligrams of Lithium Carbonate. The doctor warned I should do regular blood work since one of the side effects is that it causes kidney failure.

The psychiatrist asked, "Have you ever considered electroshock treatment?" Was frying my brain the solution to ending my mental illness? The mental health unit at the hospital was the place I ran to hide from my demons; however, when I returned home, my problems were there waiting for me. My problems were my demons and I could no longer run from them. As for me being bipolar, and consuming Lithium, I threw the drugs away. I would like to keep my kidneys thank you very much. Possible kidney failure? The side effect is worse than my diagnosis.

The incident with Sharon happened on the 4th of August and as of August 17th Sharon had not been arrested. I called the station to inform them of Sharon's address. The officer said that they had insufficient policemen to arrest Sharon. I bet if I assaulted someone, an officer would arrive at my home to arrest me. The excuse was unbelievable. But on August 19th, Sharron was arrested and made bail. She posted pictures of her and Loyd on Facebook. My mother, one of her friends on Facebook, showed support and liked her photos. I had lost all hope for humanity.

The only people I spoke to were my therapist and Camila. My therapist got paid to listen to my sob story, I was her job. Camila referred to me as her associate or neighbor. She never acknowledged me as her friend.

Camila said to me once, "I'm not you, someone who can't handle life and throws themselves in the loony bin for every little thing."

I attended an outpatient group therapy after I got discharged from the hospital. I felt out of place since most of the members attending had a problem with substance abuse. I resigned from the group. I had various problems; however, substance abuse was not one of them. That year 2017, the doctor labeled me with bipolar depressive disorder to add to the disorders I already had.

I was exhausted from wallowing in self-pity. I spoke to my father from the Virgin Island, Saint Thomas about how I felt. I had no job, friends, or my son to hold on to. My father discussed sending me a plane ticket to return; however, he stated, I would have to leave my son and everything behind. My father emphasized the fact that what I had was not a life. He continued to say that when I grew old, I would be unable to collect a retirement check. My father suggested I look at my situation in a positive way. My father wanted me to focus on me. He stressed that I could obtain two jobs if desired since my son was not with me. My father mentioned I would also miss the opportunity to see my grandmother before she died.

I called my grandmother in Dominica after my father and I ended our call. My grandmother said she lights a candle in church for me every Sunday. My aunt also mentioned I was in her prayers. These are the reasons why I believe I am alive today.

I bought the book called *You are a Badass* on my thirty-fifth birthday.

In her book, page twelve, the author Jen Sincero notes, "You need to go from wanting to change your life to deciding to change your life."

I realized life was passing me by. Something had to change for me to receive a different outcome. I threw away my prescription pills. I wanted to break free of my demons, my mental illness. I wanted to make sense of my past. I sat on my couch with the television off and had the opportunity to reflect in this empty apartment I called home. I read the book and something positive happened on my thirty-fifth birthday.

What happened on my thirty-fifth birthday? I opened my eyes. I woke up. I decided to let go and stop living in the past. I realized my life was not crazy. I was crazy. I was crazy for allowing my mental illness to bully me. I was labeled disabled when I was quite able. I learned to alter my way of thinking and stopped feeling sorry for myself. Every year I was faced with obstacles and challenges, whether it be relationship or financial. I could make excuses for why I fail to have what I want in life; however, I was my own worst enemy.

Who am I to say that one should not consume prescription drugs to treat mental illness? I am not a doctor. I can only say that prescription drugs were not what helped me. I helped myself. Take Tylenol as an example. Though Tylenol may relieve a headache, Tylenol will not eliminate what caused the headache and the headache will keep returning. I discovered what caused my mental illness. It was the everyday stress which is a fact of life. I presumed I could escape life and abandon my problems at the mental health unit at the hospital; however, my problems awaited me as soon as I returned home. The bills, unpaid debts, and responsibilities were still there. My demons bullied me when dark times approached. I called my mental illness demons since demons attack when you are weak, vulnerable, and in a fragile state of mind.

I felt better at the mental health unit since I was not alone. I saw people with real problems restrained and cast out from the outside world. I remembered consuming seven pills a day as they gradually reduced my dosage to three pills a day and I still felt depressed. I felt better when I went to the gym, painted, attended church service, or engaged in something like work. I was distracted from the harsh realities of life. I researched quotes from inspirational authors like Helen Keller, the first death and blind person to earn a bachelor of art degree. She worked on behalf of others living with disabilities.

I wrote a quote of my own. "If you want a healthy life, surround yourself with positive people. Refrain from prescription drugs for a better mood."

Drugs cannot alter your way of thinking, only you can. I realized the choices I made had consequences and led me to where I am right now.

Since 2018,, my thoughts have been of ways to grow and improve rather than harm myself. I have not consumed prescription drugs for years or been hospitalized for mental health reasons. I painted my wall with affirmations to help me stay positive.

In February 2020, I received a letter from the Social Security Administration stating that I am no longer eligible to receive social security income. Social Security concluded after an assessment that I was not disabled; however, I had the right to appeal the decision. I appealed the decision as I was comfortable with that kind of life. I was also in need of income to pay bills. A friend of mine said that God closed this door and he was going to open new doors for me. I asked myself why should I fight to be kept on disability? Why do I limit myself? I was motivated and wanted to look for full time employment when everything changed. God tested my faith and just when I felt normal again, I had to face the "New Normal."

CHAPTER 27

# *The New Normal*

"Life is a succession of lessons
which must be lived to be understood."
— *Helen Keller; American author,
disability rights advocate and lecturer.*

*N*othing was normal about the year 2020. I thought the world would end. That year, Pandemic COVID-19, coronavirus left the world at God's mercy. The president and the government demanded that people should remain home to be safe. The media counted deaths more than they counted their blessings and I prayed without ceasing. I spoke to God and I said if this is the end of the world then I have not lived at all. I wasted my years and took life for granted.

The rest of the world lived the way I lived for a long time, in self-isolation. The world called it social distancing, self-quarantine. This was new to the world; however, this has been my life for years. I alienated myself from family and turned away from friends. I believed the solution was worse than the problem. The fear of getting infected with the virus was worse than the virus. My depression and anxiety increased from watching the news. I was unable to sleep and cried myself to sleep for a few nights.

Men stated that this was God's plague upon the world. but the Bible stated that men would bring their own destruction. People hurt each other. I saw a video where a man hoarded masks and coughed on a group of FBI agents. I read on social media that a woman purposely coughed on thirty-five hundred dollars' worth of groceries at a grocery store. All the food was thrown out. Was it God? No, people hurt each other with their wicked ways. A sixth-grade teacher discussed with students that she believes they should cough on Donald Trump. Yes, the Fifth Amendment gives people the legal right to have their own voice, to say what they please; however, wishing bad for another person is not the answer. Children should be taught proper safety measures and to help each other during a crisis. I refrained from watching the news for my own positive mental state of mind.

I looked and listened for signs of hope. People also spread kindness while the virus spread. I read that Tyler Perry bought groceries for elderly shoppers at 73 stores across his hometown in Atlanta and in New Orleans. That was God working through Tyler Perry. This man is the icon and success today because he is a selfless child of God.

How has the coronavirus pandemic affected me? Well, my son presumed nothing had changed.

My son said, "You hibernate every winter mommy."

In the book of Proverbs 6 in the Bible, God said we should be wise like the ants. The ants collect food and store it in their holes to prepare for winter. I was confined to my home and tried not to be glued to the news. I stole a glimpse of sunshine on sunny days, bought food and household products, then stayed home for weeks. I gained ten pounds since I had been inactive from lack of exercise.

The world was on pause with a global shutdown that placed stress on the economy. Restaurants, stores, libraries, barber shops, schools, churches and everything was closed which raised panic in everyone. My biggest stressor was not being able to have my son with me. My son had not visited my home in four to five months as my son's father was concerned about the safety of his household. He mentioned to the police that he was purposefully violating the court order. I tried to compromise and reasoned with him, but he stated he wanted his family to be safe. We all wanted to be safe in this crisis; though I believed some people used the pandemic situation to their advantage.

My son's plan to go to the trampoline park and bowling alley had been altered due to quarantine; nevertheless, he was fortunate. My son had a computer, PlayStation and Xbox One for entertainment. My son was in his own world. Some children were not as fortunate as they missed out on education. Parents became teachers and some parents worked from home.

My therapist and vocational worker worked from home and made phone call appointments to clients. They called me every week to find out how miserable I was. I wished I got paid to sit with my child at home while I made calls to clients. The only work I did was to maintain my seventy-five-gallon fish tank. I found the fish hobby to be relaxing.

I felt lonely, still everyone I brought into my life was toxic. My failed relationships of damaged goods and family that was distant before the coronavirus. I was scared of my own thoughts and where they would lead me. Deaths increased and I believed the news purposely installed fear in people. I felt my mental state was not important enough to save a bed for me at the psych ward. The hospital barely had beds for COVID-19 patients.

People were out of work for a while and I was scared to work. Nursing homes reported having many positive cases. I chose to remain home given my history of asthma and the fact that I am pre-diabetic. I realized the future was not promised, and I thanked God I opened two gifts every morning which were my eyes. You would think at a time like this people would turn to God; however, people turned to toilet tissue, protests, arson, robbery, vandalism and unjust deaths. People wanted to be heard and demanded change. What does change look like anyway? We should be the change the world needs. We create the world we live in. I wanted to change; therefore, I worked on myself.

I rejoined Facebook and reconnected with my family during the pandemic. I video chatted on WhatsApp with my aunt, grandma, and texted those people I had shunned. The days were short and the nights were cold. I was unable to catch a break from cable television as I was reminded of deaths even on commercials. I uninstalled cable and I kept the internet to watch series on Netflix to escape the harsh realities of the world.

The world panicked and was filled with fear and anxiety. I decided, as I drew breath, I would not just have an idea, rather, act on the idea of writing a book. I placed my focus on this therapeutic exercise and reflected on my life. I typed a chapter a day of my crazy life during quarantine. I learned to value life. I remembered how I took life for granted by wanting to end my life. I would have missed out on a lot. I would have never known what the food at the restaurant Applebee's Grill and Bar tastes like. I would have never gone to Creatures Plus Aquarium to see the amazing, rare fish and reptiles selections. I would have missed out on my son developing from a teenager into a young man.

I wish I could return to do things differently; however, life is like the hand of a clock. The hands of a clock move forward, not backward. All I could do in life is move forward.

In September of 2020, I decided to stop hiding in my apartment and return to work. I received a job as a certified nursing assistant. My residents remind me that we all get old, even if some get there faster than others. You will never know what card life will deal you. I often worked on the Alzheimer's unit and I take life one day at a time. I decided that life is what you make it and I am going to continue to live "My Crazy Life."

# *Acknowledgements*

$\mathcal{S}$omeone once said that we have to grow through what we go through. The writing of *My Crazy Life* has been a time for growth for me. I would like to take the time to acknowledge some people for their help and support.

Without God I would not have the courage and confidence to write this book. Writing about my life felt like I was living life twice. God held my hand when I had given up.

Special thanks for the patience, time and devotion of the team at Stillwater River Publications for the professional editing, design and making this book possible.

How can I forget Abdu Niang? I am grateful for the numerous times he brought me food during the coronavirus pandemic while I was on quarantine. A pack of Ramen noodles was difficult to find during that time.

Mohammed Sanyang, thank you for the countless times you placed money into my account. The world needs more kind people like you.

Thanks to Dr. Phillip C. McGraw, Ph.D. for writing the book, *Self Matters*. Your book has helped me more than my eight years of therapy and has taught me how to find my authentic self. You led me to find my passion, my passion for writing.

To Jen Sincero. Your book, *You Are a Badass* has been a wakeup call for me. Your book inspired me to write my own book. I thought about writing my story, but never acted on it. Thank you.

To my son, my reason to live. Thanks for believing in me and helping me with the computer. I wrote a book when I barely spoke English.

# Author's Notes

The names in this book have been changed to protect the privacy of individuals. This is not an autobiography but a memoir. This book contains selected chapters of my life experience, how they had an impact on my life, and lessons I have learned.

In order to get to your destination in life, you have to know where you are first. I did not like where I was in life and wanted to know what brought me to where I am. I revisited the past.

I thought of all the crazy aspects of my life that I could now laugh about. I wrote a book called *My Crazy Life* that I hope you enjoy.

# About the Author

*A*isha P. Felix is the proud mother of a son whom she tiptoes to hug. She was born in the United States Virgin Islands and was raised in the Commonwealth of Dominica West Indies.

Aisha has compassion for the elderly and had a rewarding job as a Certified Nursing Assistant at the Woonsocket Health and Rehabilitation Center. A resident once called her an angel without wings. When Aisha is not working or journaling, she maintains a seventy-five-gallon fish tank.

Aisha enjoys baking, writing, spending time with her son, and watching the Lifetime Movie Network and Netflix.

Aisha believes Maya Angelou when she said, "There is no greater agony than bearing an untold story inside you."

*My Crazy Life* is her first book. Aisha began typing her story during quarantine as a therapeutic project to help understand her life and learn how to improve in the future.

Aisha currently lives in Woonsocket Rhode Island. She encourages readers to connect with her about her book on Facebook and Facebook Messenger.

Made in the USA
Middletown, DE
23 December 2021

56733363R00094